AGRICULTURAL LAW

Advising the Farmer
and
Country Landowner

AGRICULTURAL LAW

Advising the Farmer
and
Country Landowner

Second Edition

by

Graham Smith
MA, LLB (Cantab)

Solicitor and Partner with Roythorne & Co

CLT PROFESSIONAL PUBLISHING
A DIVISION OF CENTRAL LAW TRAINING LTD

Published by:
CLT Professional Publishing
A Division of Central Law Training Ltd
Wrens Court
52-54 Victoria Road
Sutton Coldfield
Birmingham
B72 1SX

ISBN 1 85811 153 3

Typeset by Cheryl Zimmerman
Printed in Great Britain by Redwood Books Ltd

Contents

Table of Cases

Table of Legislation

Introduction

The aim of the book is to provide an aide memoire for lawyers in general practice and other professional advisers with agricultural clients. Some farmers and country landowners may also find it of interest. It is intended to highlight problems but not to provide a comprehensive statement. It is assumed that when a problem has been highlighted the reader will refer to the appropriate text books or take specialist advice. Some European Union material is reproduced because it is not generally available in convenient form.

The book is in five sections:

1. an analysis of the various possible arrangements for the occupation of land;
2. an outline of the provisions of the Common Agricultural Policy which need to be borne in mind;
3. a consideration of social and environmental matters;
4. a look at animal health and particularly BSE;
5. a miscellany of tax points of particular relevance to farmers and country landowners.

Acknowledgements

I would like to thank:

Julia and Guy for putting up with repeated and extended absences during the production of the book.

Joyce for the Herculean task of typing.

My colleagues at Roythorne & Co and in Agrilaw for help in discussion and clarification. Any imperfections are mine and not theirs.

Simon Mountjoy of Brown & Co who produced the prototype on which the Notes on Timing are based.

The publishers, for guidance, encouragement and bringing the book to fruition.

Graham Smith

PART I

Possible Arrangements for the Occupation of Land

Arrangements for the occupation of land can be classifed as follows:

- Unprotected occupation rights based simply on a contract between the parties
- Tenancies of dwellings
- Business tenancies under the Landlord and Tenant Act 1954 ("the 1954 Act")
- Tenancies ("1986 Act tenancies") under the Agricultural Holdings Act 1986 ("the 1986 Act")
- Farm Business Tenancies under the Agricultural Tenancies Act 1995 ("the 1995 Act").

Otherwise the occupier may be in possession as a trespasser; possibly acquiring a prescriptive title.

These are considered in turn.

Unprotected occupation rights, 1986 Act tenancies and farm business tenancies are considered in most detail as these are the arrangements of most importance in connection with farmland. Cottage lettings and licences and business tenancies under the 1954 Act are not considered in detail.

CHAPTER 1

Unprotected Occupation Rights

These are contractual arrangements which are not affected by any statutory security of tenure or compensation provisions. The contract between the parties will contain all the terms of the relationship.

They can be classified under a number of broad headings:

- Arrangements for non business use
- Licences without consideration
- Arrangements giving occupation rights as subsidiary to another purpose
- Arrangements when there is no intention to create a tenancy
- Non-exclusive licences
- Tenancies at will created after 1 September 1995

Arrangements for non business use

A letting for personal use and enjoyment will not attract security of tenure under either the 1986 Act or the 1995 Act. It is only business arrangements that are covered.

Licences without consideration

Licences without consideration are not covered either by the 1986 Act or the 1995 Act. However some consideration (even if very small) will make the arrangements protected unless (in the case of a letting after 1 September 1995) the arrangement constitutes a tenancy at will. The cases are decided under the rules now contained in the 1986 Act but the rationale applies equally to the 1995 Act.

In the following cases it was held that the occupation was not protected.

Goldsack v Shore [1950] 1 All ER 276
A tenancy at will or licence to graze sheep was granted "without valuable consideration". The Court of Appeal held that, if there was no consideration, the 1986 Act did not apply.

Colchester BC v Smith [1991] 2 All ER 29 Ch D
A landowner allowed a person to occupy farmland rent free for some nine months. It was held to be a gratuitous licence, not protected by the 1986 Act.

Protection was granted in the following cases.

Verrall v Farnes [1966] 2 All ER 808 Ch D
Verrall allowed Farnes into occupation for a rent free trial period. The court held that he was a protected tenant.

Holder v Holder [1968] 1 All ER 665
Father allowed his son to farm the farm for a payment of about £2 per acre. The court held that a protected tenancy had been created.

Mitton v Farrow (1980) 255 EG 449
Farrow was allowed into occupation rent free to clear the land. It was held that a protected tenancy had been created.

Collier v Hollinshead (1984) 272 EG 941
Mother let a farm to her son for payments far below market rent. It was held that the son had a protected tenancy.

Padbury v York (1990) 41 EG 65
By an arrangement between father and son, the son farmed his father's land, paying the father a figure calculated on an acreage basis by reference to the rent of another farm. It was held that the son had acquired a secure tenancy.

Arrangements giving occupation rights as subsidiary to another purpose

Several cases have arisen where persons were let into occupation of property as part of another transaction. Generally they have not been treated as tenants.

Examples are the following cases:

Walters v Roberts (1980) 41 P & CR 210
The purchaser under a sale contract was allowed into possession. It was held that this was a licence to occupy which should not be treated as a tenancy as it would be "radically different".

Dockerill v Fitzpatrick (1989) 02 EG 75
An option to purchase was exercised but completion never took place. The option holder was also tenant but his tenancy was terminated. It was held that he had no secure right of occupation as a potential purchaser.

Rowan v Dann (1991) EGCS 19
There was a joint venture and it was held that any land occupation rights granted survived or fell with the joint venture. In fact the joint venture failed and the occupation rights therefore had to be given up.

Arrangements where there is no intention to create a tenancy

Where there is no intention to create a tenancy there have been several cases where payment of rent has not led to an arrangement such as would be covered by the 1986 Act or (now) the 1995 Act. None of these however is agricultural and it is not certain that they would apply in an agricultural context.

For example:

Clarke v Grant [1949] 1 All ER 768
Rent paid, after notice to quit, and accepted in error did not lead to the grant of a new tenancy.

Longrigg Burrough and Trounson v Smith (1979) 251 EG 847
The defendant held over on termination of a business tenancy. Rent was paid. A new tenancy would have been protected by the Rent Acts. The plaintiffs tried to negotiate possession in the meantime. The defendant claimed a new tenancy. It was held that no new tenancy had been created.

Cardiothoracic Institute v Shrewdcrest Ltd [1986] 3 All ER 633
Business tenants held over after a non-secure lease expired. It was intended to apply to the court for further exclusion but no application was ever made. It was held that there was no intention to grant a new protected tenancy.

On the whole the agricultural cases have been more strictly viewed. *Secretary of State for Social Services v Beavington* (1982) 262 EG 551 is an agricultural case where security applied. There Ministry approval was obtained to a 364 day "licence". A new licence was granted without obtaining a further consent. It was held that the occupier was protected.

Similar points arose in *Bedfordshire County Council* v *Clarke* (1974) 230 EG 1587.

Certainly rent should not be accepted and proceedings should if necessary be started expeditiously if there is any doubt about the situation.

Non-exclusive licences

If a true non-exclusive licence is granted the arrangement made does not create a tenancy covered by either the 1986 Act or the 1995 Act. There has been a lot of litigation over the definition of a licence sufficient to lead to a tenancy.

Many of the cases derive from the Rent Acts; for example:

Antoniades v Villiers & Another [1988] 2 All ER 309
There the landlord had no intention of allowing the tenants exclusive possession and so no tenancy was created.

There are also many cases in an agricultural context, examples being the following:

Wyatt v King (1951) 157 EG 124
A publican allowed a neighbouring farmer to graze beast and take apples from his orchard. It was held by the Court of Appeal that exclusive possession had not been given and therefore the occupation was not protected.

Bahamas International Trust Co. Ltd. v Threadgold [1974] 3 All ER 881
A tenant died. Her son agreed with the landlord holdover of occupation in the farmhouse for 11 months "as caretaker" and the right to keep and milk cows on the farm for seven months. It was held that the son did not have exclusive possession.

McCarthy v Bence (1990) 17 EG 78
Under a share milking arrangement various fields were made available to the milker. The landowner reserved various rights, such as shooting, and hedge trimming. The agreement expressly stated that exclusive possession was not given. The Court of Appeal decided that the milker did not have exclusive possession and therefore a tenancy was not created.

Evans v Tompkins (1993) 33 EG 86
Mr Tompkins was permitted "to use the grass keep for cattle and some sheep and the use of the barn for keeping cattle and storing hay during

winter months". It was found that the landowner had the right to permit others to graze horses on the land. It was held that there was no grant of exclusive possession to Mr Tompkins and therefore he was not entitled to security of tenure.

Gold v Jacques Amand Ltd & Others (1992) 27 EG 140
The occupier entered the land and erected a building at his own expense. It was held that he had exclusive possession and therefore his occupation was protected.

The best rule to work on is that if the licence gives exclusive possession then it will create a tenancy. For the future this will primarily be of interest in a fiscal context. It is necessary however to bear in mind these rules in analysing arrangements entered into before 1 September 1995.

Types of non-exclusive licence

Such licences are set up in a number of different ways. They were quite commonly used to avoid the security of tenure given by the 1986 Act and will still be popular as providing a way to protect the landowner's tax position or where a tenant does not wish to sublet. Great care is essential in setting up the agreement. It is also essential to ensure that the parties understand the agreement and will operate it in practice. If a contracting agreement is set up and the landowner demands "rent" the position may be severely prejudiced. The landowner's occupation must be more than nominal. A tax case was *Russell v Hird* (1983) STC 541 where the court held that the purchasers of standing timber were occupying the land to the exclusion of the landowner.

The situation regarding grazing is also important. A landowner may need to be in occupation of grassland, especially if he wishes to claim agricultural relief on a home occupied with it.

The cases are quite old:

McKenna v Herlihy (1920) 7TC 620
The owner was held to be in occupation where land was let for seasonal grazing.

Donald v Thomson (1922) SC 237
Again the owner rather than the occupier of grassland was treated as being in occupation.

CIR v Forsyth-Grant (1943) SC 369
The owner who undertook fencing and fertilising grassland was held to be in occupation.

Mitchell v IRC (1943) SC 380
The tenant who undertook all husbandry acts and was entitled to do more than just graze the land was held to be in occupation.

The CLA has suggested that it may now be safest to have an agreement for the sale of grass as a profit a prendre. Their booklet *Profit of Pasturage* published December 1995 includes a useful precedent.

Common non-exclusive licences in the agricultural context arise as follows.

Partnerships
Where a partner owns land and allows it to be farmed by a partnership including himself a non-exclusive licence arises.

> The leading case is *Harrison-Broadley* v *Smith* [1964] 1 All ER 876 decided by the Court of Appeal. As both partners were occupying, the licence was non-exclusive.

This assumes that no rent is paid to the landowner (although he may be entitled to an extra profit share).

If a rent is included in the partnership accounts then a tenancy arises. In *Rye* v *Rye* [1962] 1 All ER 146 it was held that two persons cannot let to themselves. However in *Joseph* v *Joseph* [1966] 3 All ER 486 Lord Denning indicated that a lease by A and B to AB and C as partners "was perfectly good" although AB and C were beneficially entitled to the freehold.

For the moment therefore it is assumed (although not authoritatively decided) that one person can let to himself and another. The consequences of this are considered further when we look at notices.

The main problem with partnerships is each party's concern about potential liability to third parties but a partnership may be necessary if substantial capital is to be provided by the non-landowning partner.

Share farming agreements
This type of agreement originated in New Zealand and Australia and has been imported to the United Kingdom. The essence of the agreement is that two separate businesses are carried on on the same land, which is a concept which we in the United Kingdom and the British courts are likely to find hard to understand. Assuming it works, occupation is non-

exclusive because both parties are entitled to occupy. There is probably not a problem but it has to be said that these arrangements have not been extensively litigated and there may therefore be some danger. The best explanation of these arrangements (including precedents) is in the CLA's publication *Share Farming: the Practice – with Model Form of Agreement* (3rd ed) by Stratton Sydenham and Baird. After initial doubts, the Revenue has now accepted that both parties may be in occupation.

Contracting and farm management agreements

Under these agreements a landowner employs a farmer to manage or do the work on the farm. The crops at all times belong to the landowner and the landowner must have a degree of risk although the profit can be shared between the landowner and the farmer. Provided these agreements are properly drawn up and adhered to they do not create security of tenure. Depending on the payment schedule the contractor may be at risk in the event of the landowner's insolvency.

Tenancies at will created after 1 September 1995

These are likely to arise where a person is permitted to enter on land by an informal arrangement without payment of rent. Payment of rent under an informal arrangement is likely to lead to a periodic tenancy. A tenancy at will can be created expressly even with payment of rent but such tenancies are likely to be rare.

CHAPTER 2

Tenancies of Dwellings

It is possible that a dwelling let as an agricultural holding can be subject to agricultural holdings legislation *Blackmore* v *Butler* [1954] 2 All ER 403 – an unusual case where a cottage was let separately to the holding (to the same tenant) for occupation by an agricultural worker.

In connection with dwellings the provisions of the Rent Act 1977 and the Housing Act 1988 may result in some protected residential tenancies.

Where an agricultural worker occupies a cottage as a term of his employment protection under the Rent (Agriculture) Act 1976 or the Housing Act 1988 may apply. In particular a letting at a rent of less than £250 per annum will be protected. Housing Act 1988 Schedule 1 paragraph 3 as amended.

Despite the general removal of notice requirements with effect from 28 February 1997 under the Housing Act 1996, notices will still be required for lettings to agricultural workers. Forms of notice are set out in the Assured Tenancies and Agricultural Occupancies (Forms) Regulations 1997 No 194.

If no protection is intended, an assured shorthold letting should be considered, although the minimum rent provision must be borne in mind.

CHAPTER 3

Business Tenancies

A business tenancy arises under the Landlord and Tenant Act 1954. Examples would be a stud farm or a garden centre not subject to the agricultural rules perhaps because all the produce is bought in. If the Landlord and Tenant Act applies then one needs to bear in mind that it carries with it security of tenure arrangements, rights to compensation for improvements and rights to compensation for disturbance.

CHAPTER 4

Adverse Possession

A person may be occupying property as a trespasser. If he does this for more than 12 years the landowner's right to recover possession may be lost. *Price* v *Hartley* (1995) EGCS 74 is a case where a tenant remained in possession without paying rent for more than 12 years and thereby the landlord's right to recover possession was excluded. This was a holiday home and the tenant was uncertain who the landlord was and so paid no rent. *Colchester BC* v *Smith* referred to earlier is also a case in point although in that case the title of the original owner was in fact revived by a new agreement. Landowners need to guard against any such possibility and ensure that their estates are properly managed.

CHAPTER 5

1986 Act Tenancies

Nothing in the 1995 Act alters the general position on existing 1986 Act tenancies. Moreover, new succession tenancies can still be granted under the 1986 Act. Accordingly, the arrangements under the 1986 Act will remain important for the foreseeable future.

This chapter will consider these arrangements in the following order:

> What is an agricultural holding?
>
> Security of tenure – the basic rules
>   – exceptions
>
> The detailed implications of a secure 1986 Act tenancy.

What is an agricultural holding?

> For the purposes of the 1986 Act an agricultural holding means "the aggregate of the land (whether agricultural land or not) comprised in a contract for an agricultural tenancy." (s 1(1) 1986 Act). It is interesting that the land does not have to be agricultural.

It covers the whole of the land comprised in the letting subject to exceptions not affecting its character which is let for use as agricultural land (subs 2). It is therefore the overall character that is important.

The land has to be used for a trade or business not simply for pleasure (subs 4). A field let for grazing by the tenant's children's pony and not used for a trade or business will not be an agricultural holding because non-business user is not covered by the 1986 Act.

If the land is not an agricultural holding the 1986 Act does not apply.

Distinction between agricultural and business tenancy
The line between an agricultural and business tenancy is sometimes hard to define.

A *garden centre* may be an agricultural holding although much of the produce is bought in. In *Short* v *Greeves* (1988) 8 EG 109 the Court of Appeal held that a garden centre was an agricultural holding although the home grown agricultural content represented only 40% of total turnover. There had been a significant increase in bought in produce after the tenancy began. Similarly in *Gold* v *Jacques Amand Ltd & Others* (1992) 27 EG 140 a wholesale bulb grower selling 15%-20% of produce grown on the six acres holding was covered by the 1986 Act.

The position regarding *camp sites* would be similar. The answer probably depends on the principal use.

A *stud farm* would not be an agricultural holding because it is not used for agriculture. Horses are not livestock and therefore the land is not being used for the breeding and keeping of livestock under section 96(1). However, that section provides that the use of land as grazing land does constitute agricultural use and so the ancillary grazing land could be an agricultural holding. It is best to prepare the agreement bearing in mind the statutory requirements both for agricultural and for business tenancies.

Security of tenure – the basic rules

The principal reason for the introduction of farm business tenancies was the concern with security of tenure expressed by landowners. A letting covered by the 1986 Act unless it fell within one of the exceptions gave security of tenure and it is therefore necessary to look at what lettings are covered.

The effect of sections 2 and 3 of the 1986 Act was that a tenancy for less than a year, a periodic tenancy, and a tenancy for two years or more were all subject to the security of tenure provisions of the 1986 Act. Licences were also converted under section 2. However only licences conferring exclusive possession were converted; non-exclusive licenses were not covered.

Exceptions to security of tenure rules

There were certain exceptions to the rules. The importance of these for the future is in making sure that the arrangement under consideration falls fairly within one of the exceptions and did not create a secure 1986 Act tenancy.

Gladstone v Bower

Gladstone v *Bower* tenancies are based on the case of *Gladstone* v *Bower* [1960] 2 QB 384. This was a letting for a fixed term of more than one and less than two years. It did not attract security of tenure because it fell between sections 2 and 3. The suggestion that such a letting was protected under the 1954 Act was refuted by the Court of Appeal in *EWP Limited* v *Moore* [1992] 1 All ER 880. On the face of it therefore if a *Gladstone* v *Bower* arrangement was entered into it did not result in any form of security of tenure.

There are one or two points to watch out for, where it is stated that the arrangement was simply a *Gladstone* v *Bower* agreement.

There had to be no guarantee that the agreement would be repeated. If the tenant held over he might well have acquired protection.

There had to be more than one year of the agreement still to run when it was signed.

Keen v Holland [1984] 1 All ER 75
The agreement was signed just before it was due to expire. The Court of Appeal held that the agreement therefore operated as the grant of a tenancy for less than a year and the full security of tenure provisions applied.

Ministry approved lettings

The Minister could consent either under section 2 or under section 5 of the 1986 Act to the grant of a tenancy not attracting security of tenure.

Under section 2 the agreement had to be for less than a year. Section 2 contained a trap for the unwary.

Ashdale Land and Property Co Limited v Manners (1992) 34 EG 76
Ministry consent was obtained in accordance with the section to the grant of a licence. The licence was subsequently granted but the licensee claimed that as the licence conferred exclusive possession it in fact created a tenancy. It was held that this was so. Therefore the Ministry consent was invalid and the licensee was entitled to security of tenure.

Under section 5 the agreement had to be for not less than two nor more than five years.

Possible problems with both sections were:

Consent had to be obtained before the grant of the tenancy.

Bedfordshire County Council v Clarke (1974) 230 EG 1587
The Ministerial consent and the tenancy were both dated 9 September. The court held that it had not been shown that the consent predated the tenancy. In that case the Council went on in the following year to obtain the consent a month after the "expiry" of the previous letting (the occupier remaining in possession). They failed to document the letting at all in that year. It was held further that even if the court were wrong on the original letting the next year's arrangements gave security.

This case may no longer be good law in respect of notices following *Bedding* v *McCarthy* (1994) 41 EG 151.

There notice under an assured shorthold was served on the tenant in the morning. The tenancy agreement was signed and the tenant went into possession. The tenancy was for six months. The tenant argued:

The tenancy was for less than six months as it could not relate back to the beginning of the day. If it did relate back the notice was invalid.

The court found for the landlord. Part of a day could be ignored in establishing a letting for six months and the notice was served before the tenancy began.

The tenancy agreement must be in the correct form. It might not be fatal if the contract was signed after the occupier had gone into possession but it must have been signed and must coincide with the consent which had been obtained. See *Pahl* v *Trevor* (1992) 25 EG 130.

Sub-tenants

A sub-tenant will be protected in the usual way against his immediate landlord. Moreover he will become the head tenant if the tenant surrenders his tenancy.

However, if the head landlord serves notice to quit on the head tenant and in consequence the tenant vacates, the sub-tenant has no right to remain on the land.

Accordingly this became a much used stratagem to avoid the security of tenure granted by the 1986 Act. This method of avoidance of security of tenure was attacked in *Gisborne* v *Burton* (1988) 38 EG 129. There a husband granted a tenancy to his wife who granted a sub-tenancy on the same day. The intention was to circumvent the security of tenure provisions of the 1986 Act. It was held that the head letting was a sham and therefore the sub-tenant was fully protected notwithstanding the service of notice to quit by the head landlord on the head tenant.

The point arose again in *Sparkes* v *Smart* (1990) 2 EGLR 245, where the head tenant sublet the farm to his son. He asked the landlord's agent for consent but it was not forthcoming. Later, the head tenant arranged for his son-in-law to buy the freehold and give the head tenant notice to quit so that the farm could be sold vacant despite the son's objection. It was held that the sub-tenancy was not terminated and the son's tenancy continued. This is also an interesting example of a case where the landlord was held to acquiesce in the sub-letting. Alternatively the court said that the head tenant held the tenancy in trust for the son until an assignment or succession tenancy was possible.

Barratt v *Morgan* (1997) 12 EG 155 was a case where in the context of a family arrangement a farm was let to members of the family. Those members farmed it initially but subsequently made an arrangement with a neighbouring farmer which in the event was held to create a tenancy protected under the Agricultural Holdings Act 1986. The landlord served notice to quit on the head tenants who failed to serve a counter notice. In the Chancery Division it was held that notwithstanding the usual rule that the sub-tenancy would fall, where there was a contrived scheme to procure vacant possession, the court would not assist the landlord. In this case there was a collusive arrangement. Accordingly the sub-tenant was promoted to be head tenant.

Grazing and/or mowing agreements

Grazing and/or mowing agreements for less than a year did not attract security of tenure. They had to be for a specified period of the year and there had to be no guarantee of renewal.

Care was needed and a number of so called grazing agreements may have created tenancies. Examples of cases on this are as follows:

Brown v Tiernan (1993) 18 EG 134
A paddock was let for grazing but not for cattle when daffodils were in bloom. The occupier used the paddock throughout the year for his children's pony and the landowner did not object. It was held that the occupier had a tenancy for the whole year subject to not grazing with cattle during the daffodil season and not a seasonal tenancy. His occupation was therefore protected.

Rutherford v Maurer [1961] 2 All ER 775
A letting "for six months periods" must be a letting of at least a year and therefore protected.

The position regarding a succession of lettings was considered in *Scene Estate Ltd* v *Amos* [1959] 2 All ER325. There were 21 renewals of grazing agreements, each for three months. An expectation of renewal did not amount to a "contemplation" of occupation for more than a specified period of a year.

But where there was an understanding that the grazier would remain for "a period of years" albeit a written six months grazing agreement was completed and renewed the occupier was protected. The series of agreements completed over some 13 years were "not genuine". The signing of the last one did not constituted a surrender and regrant because it was not genuine like the others. See *Short Bros (Plant) Ltd* v *Edwards* (1979) 249 EG 539. The situation may be different where there is simply a mistake.

Cox v Husk (1976) 239 EG 123
There was a succession of grazing agreements, one of which was granted from 1 April 1970 to 31 March 1971. It was held at first instance that notwithstanding the term of the formal agreement the tenancy was in fact only for a part of a year. It was further accepted that there could be a surrender and regrant which might destroy a previous secure letting and that an incorrect agreement could perhaps be rectified.

The importance of considering in detail the exceptions to the security of tenure provisions now is so that one can check whether or not any of them applies in a particular case. Assuming that there is a secure 1986 Act tenancy what are the points which need to be borne in mind?

Terms of the agreement

The first thing to establish is what are the terms of the agreement. Often this will be obvious where there is a written agreement. In other cases, however, there will be no agreement or simply agreement as to rental and the property. In these cases section 6 of and Schedule 1 to the 1986 Act contain machinery for incorporating certain standard terms. Where there are no terms agreed it is important to consider these provisions and if appropriate serve notice under section 6.

One of the most important clauses to appear in a tenancy agreement is the clause relating to assignment and parting with possession. It is crucial to check whether or not such a clause is present. If it is not then the tenant will be able to assign his tenancy perhaps to a limited company. Accordingly a practitioner acting for the tenant should look carefully at the agreement and consider whether an assignment is possible.

It is also necessary to check whether possession can be shared for example by entering into partnership or whether only personal occupation by the tenant is possible. Often farmers farm through the medium of a limited company and it is possible that this may be a breach of the tenancy agreement. If this is likely to cause trouble then it may be worth either entering into partnership with the company if that is practicable or employing the company as contractor. The position of a company was considered in *Snell* v *Snell* (1964) 191 EG 361 where the company which had been allowed into occupation was held to be a subtenant.

When acting for a landowner with an agreement which has no ban on assignment then notice should be served under section 6 as quickly as possible. Once the notice has been served then any assignment is void.

Tenancy agreements are often lost in the mists of time. An assignment in contravention of a ban on assignment would prima facie be an irremediable breach resulting in the loss immediately of the tenancy. If there is any doubt at all about the existence of the agreement it is safer not to assign the tenancy.

It was held in *Wilson* v *Hereford and Worcester County Council* in 1991 that the assignment itself was void and therefore this consequence did not result. The *Wilson* case however was an assignment after a section 6 notice had been served and subsection (5) expressly provides for an assignment in contravention to be void.

In *Troop* v *Gibson* (1986) 277 EG 1134 where both parties assumed that there was no written agreement (but the agreement later reappeared) it was held that the landlord was estopped from serving notice to quit since the landlord had agreed there was no written agreement; however the tenant for the future would be bound by the restriction on assignment contained in the agreement.

The landlord may have acquiesceced in any arrangements made. An example is *Sparkes* v *Smart* referred to earlier.

Also, a subletting may not be regarded as an irremediable breach. See *Pennell* v *Payne*, referred to later.

The term date is important because that is the relevant date for rent review and notice to quit purposes. It is therefore necessary to try and agree when this is.

This was considered by the Court of Appeal in *J W Childers Trustees* v *Anker* (1995) EGCS 116. There had been two separate lettings but later one agreement on a rent review referring to one holding. It was held that the terms of the original agreements subsisted in respect of each area originally covered and the separate tenancies continued.

Repairs and insurance

The tenancy agreement will often specify the repair liabilities. If not, the model clauses may apply which are incorporated by section 7 of the 1986 Act. The current regulations are the Agriculture (Maintenance Repair and Insurance of Fixed Equipment) Regulations 1973 as amended.

It is appropriate to consider the tenant's position where the model clauses apply and the landlord is in breach of his repairing obligations.

Grayless v Watkinson (1990) 21 EG 163
The Court of Appeal considered such a situation. There the landlord failed to replace a barn roof which was accepted as his responsibility. The tenant did the work at a cost of almost £8,000 – under regulation 12 (2) the maximum the tenant could recover was whatever was the smaller of the rent of the holding for that year or £500 (now increased to £2,000). It was held that the tenant could recover £500 per year until the full amount was recovered; effectively, therefore, an interest free loan to the landlord!

Tustian v Johnston [1993] 2 All ER 673
The landlord failed to do any repairs despite receiving insurance monies in respect of fire damage. As the tenants were impecunious, largely because of this, they obtained legal aid for an action in the Chancery Division for damages and specific performance. It was held (with some reluctance) that the actions must be stayed as the tenants had first to establish liability under the regulations by arbitration. On appeal noted at [1993] 3 All ER 534 the Court of Appeal ordered that an application for summary judgment should proceed.

Hammond v Allen [1994] 1 All ER 307
The tenant served notice under the model clauses. The holding was of 23 acres and a farmhouse which over some 30 years had fallen into disrepair. The estimated cost of the works required was £35,000. The landlords failed to serve counternotice within the one month limitation period. It was held that the landlords were not entitled to serve a counternotice out of time. Accordingly liability was established by default and the tenant was entitled to seek damages and specific performance.

In summary, it seems that the tenant should first establish liability and then sue in the courts for damages or specific performance. If he does the work at his expense he may be a long time recovering his money!

Tenant's fixtures

The tenant has a statutory right to remove tenant's fixtures given by section 10 of the 1986 Act.

When a new tenancy is being granted it is best to specify the tenant's fixtures at that time so that there is no possible argument that they belong to the landlord.

The tenant must remember to serve notice regarding the fixtures one month *before* the end of the tenancy.

Provision of fixed equipment

There is provision in section 11 of the 1986 Act for the situation where a tenant is obliged by law to have certain equipment but it is not covered under the agreement.

Many tenancy agreements will contain an obligation on the part of the tenant to comply with any legislation affecting his activities. Particularly with the tendency towards increased environmental control this obligation may be extremely onerous.

On the other hand where the agreement does not refer to this obligation those obligations may fall upon the landlord in consequence of section 11.

It may be worth referring to some ALT decisions on this point by way of example:

Hindle v Wright (1993 – ALT Western Area)
The case concerned a pig farm (of just over one acre). An effluent tank was required (costing about £34,000). An order was made.

Rawsthorne v Carnforth Motor Company Ltd (1993 – ALT Western Area)
This was a direction by consent. A slurry tank was to be provided by the landlord subject to a contribution of £1,500 by the tenant.

Sutcliffe v Lawrence (1993 – ALT Western Area)
There was a direction for a new slurry tank.

In view of the likely cost of this type of work such an order is a very serious matter for landlords and section 11 should always be considered.

Arbitration as to rent

Section 12 and Schedule 2 of the 1986 Act set out the procedure for rent arbitration.

It is not appropriate here to consider in detail the rent review procedure. However it is appropriate to highlight some potential problems and areas of difficulty.

As the rent can only be reviewed every three years sometimes a small review will hold the level for a three year period.

A change in the holding, for example the surrender of a cottage and a rent adjustment, may well mean that no review can take place for the following three years. Paragraph 6 of Schedule 2 to the 1986 Act (relating to boundary variations) is fairly restrictive. This point was litigated in *Mann* v *Gardner* (1990) 61 P & CR 1. There the surrender of a cottage and .603 acre with a rent reduction of £100 started the three year period again.

As usual in agricultural holdings matters it is essential that the time limits are exactly followed. The review notice must be served at the appropriate time and the arbitrator must be appointed or the President applied to before the review date. There is always a temptation to leave negotiations until the last minute in case rent levels change. The risk with this is that the appointment of the arbitrator may not go ahead within the appropriate time scale and unless another notice has been served the rent review may in consequence be deferred for two years.

It is sometimes thought that once a notice to review the rent has been served it can be withdrawn by the party serving it. This is not so and either party can use the notice.

Where the reversion has been severed there may well be difficulties on rent review since all the landlords have to join in to serve a notice of rent review. It is a matter of good practice that when the reversion is severed if the tenant will agree it is desirable for a formal apportionment to take place so that effectively the tenant has separate tenancies. The tenant however will be reluctant to agree to this. It could weaken his family's position on a succession claim and might even lead to a surrender and regrant possibly resulting in two farm business tenancies instead of one 1986 Act tenancy.

J W Childers Trustees v *Anker* referred to previously is a case where rent review was considered. It was held that one could consider marriage value both for the tenant and other possible tenants but not for comparables. Also payments under a management agreement with the NCC (now English Nature) would be taken into account.

Notice to quit

The security of tenure provisions operate by imposing restrictions on the effect of notices to quit. Section 25 of the 1986 Act amends the common law rule as to the length of the notice to quit and is self explanatory. The usual rule is 12 months from the end of the then current year of the tenancy unless there is a provision for short notice in the agreement or the tenant is insolvent. Many tenancy agreements contain a provision for short notice for non-agricultural use.

The structure of the security of tenure provisions is that a tenant has the right to serve a counter notice within one month of the giving of a notice to quit and in that event the notice to quit has no effect unless the Agricultural Land Tribunal consents (s 26). A counter notice cannot be served in the Cases set out in Part 1 Schedule 3 to the 1986 Act. Section 27 contains the grounds on which the Tribunal shall consent although subsection (2) provides that they shall not consent if "a fair and reasonable landlord would not insist on possession".

If Case D is used by the landlord the tenant has an opportunity to serve a counter notice under section 28.

There are many tribunal decisions on section 27 and each case turns very much on its merits. Whether or not this route is followed usually depends on the degree of antipathy between the parties and the depth of their respective pockets.

In *National Trust* v *Knipe* (1997) EGCS 73 an argument that a notice to quit a farm including a dwelling was invalid unless it contained the warning notices prescribed by the Protection from Eviction Act 1977 was rejected by the Court of Appeal.

A number of points may usefully be amplified in connection with notices to quit.

Notice to quit part
At common law a notice to quit part of a holding is ineffective. Notice to quit part will only be effective therefore where:

- There is a provision in the tenancy agreement permitting it; or
- Section 31 of the 1986 Act applies; or
- The reversion has been severed (section 140 Law of Property Act 1925).

This arises most often where planning permission has been obtained on part of the holding and the landlord wants to sell that part to a developer. Where there is no express provision in the tenancy agreement section 31 is unlikely to help because of the restrictive purposes for which land can be recovered under that section. The developer is usually not keen to rely on his ability to obtain possession (perhaps almost two years in future) and wants the vendor of the land with planning permission to give vacant possession. The tenant can sometimes therefore negotiate for significant compensation for giving immediate possession. In drafting a new agreement on behalf of a landlord appropriate provision should always be made if possible for notice to quit part in the event of the land being required for non agricultural use. Severance of the reversion was considered in *Persey* v *Bazley* (1983) 267 EG 519. There planning permission was obtained for residential development of about two acres. The freehold of the area with planning permission was conveyed to bare trustees for the original owners. The Court of Appeal held that a transaction of this nature did not constitute a severance.

This was considered further in *John* v *George* (1995) 22 EG 146; (1996) 8 EG 140 (CA). There the freehold of part was conveyed to trustees on trust for the daughter of the owners of the remainder of the farm upon attaining 18 years or finishing full time education. Despite this creating (inadvertently) a resulting trust for the donors pending the contingency being satisfied, it was held that the severance was sufficient. Although the case was appealed, this point was not argued on appeal.

It may be helpful to comment on various of the specific cases where a counter notice cannot be served.

Case B

All of the land the subject of the notice must be *required*; not necessarily by the landlord. The leading case, although turning partly on the express wording of the agreement in that case is *Paddock Investments Ltd* v *Lory* (1975) 236 EG 803. The case demonstrates the importance of wide enough wording being inserted in a tenancy agreement.

John v *George* is an interesting case where the Court of Appeal held that the landlord was stopped from relying on Case B to recover possession. There the tenant had agreed not to object to the landlord's planning application on the basis that new buildings would be provided.

In the event planning permission for the new buildings was not forthcoming but the landlord still sought to recover possession of the old buildings.

Case D

If the landlord serves a valid notice to pay the tenant must pay the rent within the two month period. There are many cases on this. For example:

Dickinson v Boucher (1983) 269 EG 1159

The rent on the notice to pay was stated as £650 not £625. It was held that the notice was bad.

Sloan Stanley Estate Trustees v Barribal (1994) 44 EG 237

The landlord served notice to pay £10,500. The tenant deducted the landlord's portion of drainage rates but had not actually paid the rates to the drainage authority at the time. The court held that the tenant had not complied with the notice and therefore the notice to quit must have effect.

Hannaford v Smallacombe (1993) EGCS 204

The tenant delivered the rent cheque in time but it bounced. Although it was subsequently cleared it was held that payment had not been made within the time limit.

Luttenberger v North Thoresby Farms Limited (1993) 17 EG 102

In this case the rent cheque was only signed by one signatory whereas two were required. The second signature being added out of time the payment had not been made in time. The case is salutary reading showing how wrong things can go! Interestingly an over deduction of £8.50 landlord's drainage rate was not regarded as fatal.

Beevers v Mason (1978) 248 EG 781

Where the rent was usually paid and accepted by cheque the date of posting was the date of payment.

Where a dwelling house is included in the letting the name and address of the landlord must be included in the agreement. If not the rent is not due until notice thereof has been served on the tenant. Consequently a notice to pay would be ineffective. Section 48 Landlord and Tenant Act 1987.

In *Cambridgeshire CC v Faulkner* (1992) 01 EG 101 and *Dallhold Estates (UK) Pty Ltd v Lindsey Trading Ppts Ltd* (1994) 17 EG 148 it was held that such notice had to be separately given. In *Rogan & Another v Woodfield Building Services Ltd* (1995) 20 EG 132, however, where the landord's name and a UK address appeared on the face of the lease it was held by the Court of Appeal that no separate notice was required and *Dallhold* was distinguished.

It cannot be stressed too strongly that the tenant confronted with a notice to pay must act well within the time limit and with great care. The sort of brinkmanship shown in many of the cases is foolhardy given the possibility of losing the tenancy.

If the tenant wishes to contest the subsequent notice to quit he must serve notice within one month of the notice to quit requiring arbitration. If he does not do so, even if the notice to pay was defective, if the notice to quit is valid on its face it will have effect (*Magdalen College Oxford* v *Heritage* [1974] 1 All ER 1065).

In general, if Case D is in issue it is imperative to check and watch the procedural details and time limits. Many cases are won or lost on a technicality.

Case E

An assignment of the tenancy in breach of a term of the agreement would constitute an irremediable breach save in unusual circumstances such as those in *Wilson* v *Hereford and Worcester County Council* and *Troop* v *Gibson* referred to previously. The position regarding sub-letting is different.

An interesting case on this was *Pennell* v *Payne* (1995) 6 EG 152. There a tenant entered into an arrangement with a substantial farming company which the arbitrator found had created a sub-tenancy. The head landlord served notice to quit under Case E on the grounds that he had been materially prejudiced by an irremediable breach namely the sub-letting. Interestingly the Court of Appeal held that the landlord's interest had not been materially prejudiced because if the head tenant served notice to quit the sub-tenancy would fall with the head tenancy. The only way in which the landlord could have the sub-tenant foisted upon him would be by a surrender which he could not be compelled to accept. This case reversed the previous law laid down by *Brown* v *Wilson* in 1949. This case will give some comfort to the tenant who may have sub-let inadvertently. It appeared to drive a coach and horses through Case E on the subject of sub-letting and one wonders what remedies the landlord has.

The landlord must consider his position where a tenant has sublet in breach of the tenancy agreement. He might consider forfeiture although presumably relief could possibly be granted. He might also seek an injunction.

Although not an agricultural case, the case of *Hemingway Securities Limited* v *Dunraven Limited & Another* (1995) 09 EG 322 may give some solace to landlords.

In that case surveyors held a lease which included a covenant not to underlet without consent. The tenants sub-let without consent. Jacob J granted an injunction requiring the immediate surrender of the sub-lease on the grounds that there was a plain breach of a contract by the tenant and a case of inducing or aiding a breach of contract by the sub-tenant. Furthermore the Judge was prepared to treat the covenant as a restrictive covenant and therefore binding on successors in title.

Sparkes v *Smart* referred to above is also relevant in respect of estoppel and acquiescence.

A further case on this aspect is *Wallace* v *C Brian Barratt & Son Ltd* (1997) EGCS 40. There the company was tenant of the land. The landlord argued that the arrangements made with the family partnership amounted to sharing possession which was not permitted in the tenancy agreement. The arbitrator held that the activities carried out by the partnership were as agents for the tenant and the tenant had not shared occupation. The Court of Appeal upheld this view.

Case F
Interestingly the definition of insolvency does not include the appointment of a receiver.

Case G
It is important now to remember the need for notice to be given by the representatives of the deceased tenant. In *Lees* v *Tatchell* (1990) 23 EG 62 it was held that the return of a rent demand addressed to the executors with an executors cheque was not adequate notice. The requirement of a notice was also considered in *BSC Pension Fund Trustees Ltd* v *Downing* (1990) 19 EG 87. Newspaper advertisements and a letter from solicitors saying they did not act and notifying the landlord who did were not sufficient.

Succession to tenancy

In 1976 tenants were given the opportunity for members of the family to succeed for two generations. The present legislation is set out in sections 34–59 of the 1986 Act.

On the whole the provisions are self explanatory but one or two comments may usefully be made.

Lettings covered

By section 34 succession only applies to lettings taking effect before 12 July 1984 and subsequent successions to such lettings.

The case of *Saunders* v *Ralph* (1993) 28 EG 127 is interesting. In that case it was argued that a transaction which took place in 1957 constituted a first succession as a surrender and regrant. The case arose from a succession application in 1988. The question was whether the application constituted a first succession or a second succession. It was held that the application was a first succession since the 1957 transaction was an assignment not a surrender and regrant. It was suggested *obiter* that had the 1957 transaction been a grant of a new tenancy it would have constituted a first succession. This is therefore the situation which must be watched.

Where a new succession agreement is being signed it is as well to specify whether it is a first or second succession and that the succession provisions apply for the avoidance of doubt. In any event, to ensure that the 1986 Act rules apply the parties must expressly provide for this. Otherwise a farm business tenancy will be created (s 4(1)(d) 1995 Act).

Eligible persons

Under section 35 parents, nephews and nieces and grandchildren are not eligible. There may therefore be a problem where two brothers hold a tenancy one of whom has children and one of whom does not. If the childless brother survives longer nobody will be eligible to succeed. Similarly if the grandfather lives a long time and is predeceased by his son or daughter again there may be nobody eligible to succeed. Since parents cannot succeed, if a tenancy is made over to a child, who dies unexpectedly, the tenancy may be lost. These points must be carefully considered when reviewing the succession position.

Principal source of livelihood

It is important to check this carefully. There have been many tribunal cases but the livelihood test was considered in *Littlewood* v *Rolfe* [1981] 2 All ER 51, a case brought by a young widow. "Principal source" meant 51% but it was held that what is now section 41 had a fairly wide interpretation.

Welby v Casswell (1995) 42 EG 134

The applicant was a partner who applied on his father's death. Unfortunately the business had not been trading profitably and his drawings during the relevant period were in effect substantially made up from cash introduced by the partners and others from outside sources and an increase in the bank overdraft. The Court of Appeal held that the applicant was eligible and a "purposive" approach should be adopted. The applicant here was probably fortunate and an application under section 41 should always be made.

Bailey v Sitwell (1986) 279 EG 1092
It was held that the applicant could succeed where the drawings could be shown to be from previous retained profits.

The situation should always be reviewed very carefully in structuring arrangements.

The applicant's livelihood can be derived from a larger agricultural unit, not just the holding itself.

Under section 41 the outcome has to be "fair and reasonable".

Occupation of other units
Schedule 6 Part 1 1986 Act.

The applicant's occupation of other units must be borne in mind. It is as well in each case to calculate whether or not a problem is likely to arise. Reference must be made to the Agricultural Holdings (Units of Production) Order in force at the time. Some surprising results may arise. Care should be taken to make sure so far as possible that any units are occupied merely as licensee. Such a licence should be non-exclusive to prevent a tenancy arising. The addition of the word "only" may cause problems in any event.

A farm business tenancy for less than five years (including a periodic tenancy) is disregarded but such a tenancy for longer, possibly even with a break clause, will be taken into account.

When planning for succession it is important to check on the details of all the landholdings and ensure so far as possible that the applicant will satisfy the eligibility tests.

The eligibility rules must be satisfied both at the date of death and at the date of the hearing; a discretionary will may be appropriate where the tenant owns some land which the applicant is ultimately intended to inherit.

Suitability
The applicant must also be suitable. He should be able to satisfy the Agricultural Land Tribunal that he is capable of running and has sufficient finance available to run the holding.

It is desirable to review the business arrangements to make quite sure where succession is in point that everything possible has been done to ensure that the applicant is eligible and suitable.

Order of applications

Under section 42 the applicant has the opportunity to arrange the order in which the applications are heard. If there are some holdings which clearly will not constitute a commercial unit and others that will, then it could be worth putting the smaller units on first in the hope that tenancies will be obtained which will not affect the main holding.

Approach

Litigation is always uncertain and the uncertainty is increased by section 44 giving the tribunal the opportunity to confirm the notice to quit. The applicant should try and show that he has a good case morally as well as legally.

Designation

It is as well to include a designation in each tenant's will under section 39(4). This gives the tenant the choice of preferred applicant rather than the Tribunal. It has the additional advantage of leading both the tenant and his adviser to address the need for succession planning.

Application

The time limit for making an application is three months from the death of the tenant; this is now not the same as the landlord's time limit for serving a Case G notice. It is therefore essential to ascertain immediately a farmer dies whether succession is in point and to take appropriate action.

The forms appear informal but an informal approach to the application can be disastrous. The homework must be done and an effort made to make the application as thorough as possible.

Terms of tenancy

Section 47 refers to the tenancy terms. In practice where succession is granted by agreement, the agreement is usually updated. Tenantright, dilapidations, tenants fixtures and improvements should be considered.

Succession on retirement

Succession on retirement applies where the tenant is over 65 or incapacitated. Usual reasons for doing this are:

- For peace of mind and certainty.
- With a view to testing the strength of the landlord's case (although

this is rather an expensive way of doing it). The application can be discontinued at any time. Tenants sometimes start the succession procedure in the hope that it will succeed. If the application seems to be going badly then they discontinue and apply again later on or when the tenant dies. At that stage there is nothing to be lost. If the application is dismissed no further retirement notice can be served (s 51(2)). An application may still be made on death but not by the person nominated unsuccessfully (s 57(4)).

- Where the applicant hopes to expand the business in some way and thereby in future cease to derive his principal source of livelihood from the tenanted holding. If he can secure the tenancy first then he is able to expand the business without trouble in future.

Rather than rely on succession, tenants often apply to the landlord to agree to the grant of a tenancy in favour of a son or daughter. Such a request is often granted in a case where succession would otherwise be available usually in consideration of a rent increase or some other change to the tenancy. Such a course of action should always be contemplated because of the uncertainties of litigation. Following the changes to inheritance tax relief (at 100% for lettings after 1 September 1995) landlords may be more amenable to granting such requests.

The consequences of error

Layzell v Smith Morton & Long (1992) 13 EG 118
The defendant solicitors failed to claim succession for their client. It was held the applicant would have been likely to succeed (despite the need to employ his uncle and a neighbouring farmer as contractors). Damages of £344,000 were awarded on the basis that he would have to buy a farm and enter into a sale and leaseback transaction to restore his position.

Compensation for disturbance

Section 60 of the 1986 Act makes provision for payment of compensation for disturbance.

The compensation is usually five times the rent and it is not possible to contract out of payment. This usually arises where Case B applies. A claim for extra compensation must be made not less than one month before the termination of the tenancy.

Compensation for tenantright and improvements

Sections 64–69 of the 1986 Act provide for compensation for improvements carried out by the tenant.

It is important to realise that the landlord's consent is usually required in writing for the tenant to be entitled to compensation for improvements. The tenant should therefore ensure that he obtains this. Often consent is given on the basis that the improvement will be written off over a period of years. This is not however essential and section 66 of the 1986 Act contains a formula which will operate if nothing else is agreed. It is possible however that this formula would give rise to unexpected results and there is therefore a lot to be said for quantifying the payment to be made.

Section 69 applies to successive tenancies. It is really better however where there are improvements subsisting at the beginning of the tenancy carried out either by the same tenant or by a member of his family to specify these in the new tenancy agreement so that there is no room for doubt.

Compensation for dilapidations

Sections 71–73 of the 1986 Act provide for compensation to be payable to the landlord in the event of dilapidations. Notice must be served not later than one month before the end of the tenancy.

Again there is provision for successive tenancies but it is as well to record the position if a new tenancy agreement is negotiated. In all cases where a tenancy ends it is imperative to check the time limits and make sure that the appropriate claims are made within them.

Contracting out of the 1986 Act

Contracting out of the security of tenure provisions of the 1986 Act was not possible. It was tried in *Johnson* v *Moreton* [1978] All ER 37 and given short shrift by the court.

CHAPTER 6

Farm Business Tenancies

What is a farm business tenancy?

Sections 1–4 of the 1995 Act deal with this.

The Act only applies to tenancies (s 1(1)). Accordingly non-exclusive licences are not covered and will remain important. It does not apply to tenancies at will (s 38(1)).

Business condition

All or part of the land must be farmed for the purpose of a trade or business and this must have continued since the beginning of the tenancy (s 1(2)). Accordingly lettings for non business purposes are not covered. At least part of the land must continue to be farmed.

The tenancy must satisfy the agriculture condition or the notice conditions.

Agriculture condition

This means that the character of the tenancy is primarily or wholly agricultural (s 1(3)).

Notice conditions

Alternatively, the tenancy can be subject to the notice conditions, *i.e.* the parties have served notice on each other containing the information set out in section 1(4)(a) and at the beginning of the tenancy the character of the tenancy was primarily or wholly agricultural. This is presumably intended to cover the situation where a letting originally made for agricultural purposes changes its nature: for example, the changing farm shop or the diversification exercise into a safari park! The Farm Business Tenancy rules will continue to apply rather than the Landlord and Tenant Act 1954.

The requirements of the 1995 Act in respect of the form of the notice must be complied with. In addition the case law relating to service of notices will still be relevant. They have to be served on or before the day the parties sign an agreement for the tenancy or the beginning of the tenancy (whichever is earlier) (s 1(5)). Relevant cases are *Bedfordshire County Council* v *Clarke* and *Bedding* v *McCarthy* referred to above.

What is not a farm business tenancy?

1. A tenancy beginning before 1 September 1995 (s 2).
2. A tenancy granted by a contract before 1 September 1995 indicating that the 1986 Act is to apply (s 4(1)(a)).
3. A succession tenancy arising from Part IV of the 1986 Act either granted by the tribunal's direction or by consent (s 4(1)(b) (c) and (d)). Where the tenancy is granted by agreement section 4(2) prevents the parties opting into the 1986 system in a non-succession case by providing that the grant must be in a case where succession would otherwise apply. Most difficulties arise where it is intended that a succession tenancy should be granted by agreement. The first priority is that the written contract must indicate that Part IV of the 1986 Act is to apply in relation to the tenancy (s 4(1)(d)). It is section 4(2) which causes the difficulty. It was clearly intended to ensure that parties could not contract into the old system by the simple expedient of providing that Part IV was to apply. What the section appears to mean is that only a tenancy which would constitute a succession under the 1986 Act rules will be a succession tenancy and remain under the old Act. Accordingly, the rules on eligibility and suitability must be satisfied on the commencement of the new tenancy.

Some commentators feel that a direction by the tribunal is now essential on the grant of a retirement succession tenancy. On the face of it this does not appear necessary but the cautious should adopt this approach.

In the event of the death of a tenant an application for succession should be made as a matter of course. To ensure that section 37(1)(b) of the 1986 Act applies where more than one application is made and the tenancy is to be granted by agreement the other applicants should first withdraw. If a tenant has died and no application has been made within three months then any new tenancy granted cannot by definition be a tenancy operating as an agreed succession within the terms of the Act. Great care is therefore required to ensure that the provisions of the Act are met.

4. A tenancy to which the *Evesham* custom applies (s 4(1)(e)).
5. A tenancy granted where a purported variation of a 1986 Act protected tenancy has effect as an implied surrender and regrant section 4(1)(f).

Section 4(1)(f) poses considerable difficulty. In the first instance, it only applies to a "purported" variation. It is assumed that purported means something that was intended to vary the tenancy rather than trigger a surrender and regrant. On the face of it therefore it would not cover an arrangement purposely made with a view to triggering a surrender and regrant.

Where a surrender and regrant applies was considered in the case of *Friends Provident Life Office* v *British Railways Board* [1996] 1 All ER 336. It was made clear in that case that the court would lean against a change to a tenancy having effect as a surrender and regrant. However, two examples were given namely an increase in the extent of the property or an extension of the term for which the property is held.

Likewise in the case of *JW Childers Will Trustees* v *Anker*, considered earlier, the court confirmed that it felt it should not be too hasty to find that a surrender and regrant had occurred.

If any proposals are therefore put to a tenant designed to take advantage of section 4(1)(f) he should beware. If a surrender and regrant occurs and section 4(1)(f) does not apply the tenant will have a farm business tenancy and not a 1986 Act tenancy. Likewise an express surrender and regrant will substitute a farm business tenancy for a 1986 Act tenancy.

In general, arrangements which would previously have created a 1986 Act Protected Tenancy will now create a Farm Business Tenancy. Although these arrangements will not carry security of tenure there may be other problems since, where they are created informally, many of the matters which ought to have been considered will not have been dealt with.

Termination of the tenancy

Sections 5, 6 and 7 of the 1995 Act refer to the termination of farm business tenancies.

A tenancy for a term of more than two years shall continue as a tenancy from year to year unless at least 12 months but less than 24 months before the term date a written notice has been given by either party to the other of his intention to terminate the tenancy (s 5). By section 5(4) it is impossible to contract out of this provision. Accordingly the usual three month short notice clause in the event of say planning permission being obtained will not be possible.

A tenancy from year to year will only be terminable by notice to quit in writing to take effect at the end of the year of the tenancy which is given at least 12 months but less than 24 months before the date on which it is to take effect (s 6). Again by section 6(1) this takes effect notwithstanding any provision to the contrary in the tenancy.

Where there is a tenancy for more than two years with a break clause the notice operating the break must be at least 12 but less than 24 months (s 7). Once again there is no contracting out. It does not take effect in respect of a lease for lives under section 149 Law of Property Act 1925.

There is no mention of tenancies for two years or less and accordingly tenancies for a term of two years or less will expire on the term date without any notice. Periodic tenancies (other than yearly tenancies) are not covered and will therefore be subject to the usual common law rules. It will therefore be important to consider what type of tenancy is being created and what the consequences are for the notice period.

Tenant's right to remove fixtures and buildings (s 8)

The tenant has the right to remove any fixtures affixed to the holding by him and any building erected by him on the holding. The right is only exercisable while the tenant is in possession as tenant (s 8(1)). If therefore he fails to remove them during that period his right of removal ceases.

Sub-section (2) contains some exceptions namely:

1. Where the fixture was affixed or the building erected in pursuance of some obligation. It is not stated to whom the obligation is owed. It need not necessarily be the landlord.
2. To a fixture affixed or a building erected instead of some fixture or building belonging to the landlord. Interesting points could arise here if a modest traditional building is replaced by a state of the art modern building.
3. To a fixture or building in respect of which the tenant has obtained compensation under section 16 of the 1995 Act or otherwise.
4. To a fixture or building in respect of which the landlord has given his consent under section 17 of the 1995 Act on condition that the tenant agrees not to remove it and which the tenant has agreed not to remove.

There are the usual provisions for not doing any avoidable damage and making good damage done. The provision also applies to a fixture or building acquired by a tenant as well as one affixed or erected by him *i.e.* in a deal with the previous tenant. There is no contracting out and this provision takes effect notwithstanding any custom to the contrary. Furthermore there is no other right to remove fixtures. The tenant has to serve no notice of his intention to remove the fixtures and the landlord has no right to acquire them as he does under the 1986 Act.

Rent review

Sections 9–14 of the 1995 Act contain the provisions relevant to rent review.

The parties can agree:

- That the rent is not to be reviewed at all during the tenancy (s 9(a)).
- That the rent is to be varied either by a specified amount or in accordance with a formula but not subject to the exercise by any person of a value judgment (s 9(b)). Where a farm business tenancy is being substituted for a 1986 Act Tenancy consideration must be given to the rent level. As statutory reviews under 1995 Act tenancies are (at least in the short term) likely to be higher than those under 1986 Act tenancies a formula may be necessary. It may be possible to link the rent to an index of 1986 Act rents or perhaps to rent of a nearby holding or holdings. It may be possible to complete a collateral deed of covenant under which the landlord agrees to compensate the tenant for any excess of the rent over what a 1986 Act rent would have been. However, there is doubt as to its efficacy. None of these arrangements is entirely satisfactory. Section 9 of the Act provides that if a formula is adopted the rent otherwise is to remain fixed. Accordingly if the formula fails, presumably one would be left with a fixed rent tenancy. If a formula is chosen express review provisions appear to be required as section 9 disapplies the remainder of that Part of the Act.
- On what date is to be the review date for the purpose of service of rent review notices (ss 10(4) and (5)).

Section 10 provides that review notices must be served at least 12 months but less than 24 months before the review date. Even if the parties have therefore agreed the review date, there is still a requirement to serve notice. There will however be no need or opportunity to serve notice in the event of the rent being indexed.

The review date must be an anniversary of the beginning of the tenancy or such other date as the parties have agreed and if dates are not agreed cannot fall before the end of the period of three years beginning with the latest of:

- The beginning of the tenancy.
- The date from which there takes effect a direction of an arbitrator or any other person nominated by the parties for that purpose as to the rent.
- The date from which there takes effect a written agreement between the parties as to the amount of the rent.

Accordingly it seems that, unlike the 1986 Act, a rent change is not necessarily required to restart the three year period. An agreement in writing as to the rent, without any change, will suffice.

Section 11 covers the situation where the reversion is severed in order to maintain the existing review period.

Section 12 provides for arbitration. The possibilities are:

- The parties can agree on an arbitrator.
- The parties can agree on an expert.
- If neither of these has happened either party may during the period of six months ending with the review date apply to the President of the RICS to appoint an arbitrator. The application must be made before the review date. Otherwise as under the 1986 Act the opportunity for the review will be lost.

Section 13 contains guidance for the arbitrator as to how he is to determine the rent. He has to take into account "all relevant factors" (s 13(2)). Although some of the matters will be familiar some other provisions no longer appear. For example the detailed guidance as to productive capacity and related earning capacity is not repeated presumably on the basis that this is unnecessary and indeed may be inappropriate if the tenancy has largely ceased to be agricultural.

Landlords grant aided improvements are not to be disregarded.

Tenant's improvements are to be disregarded except:

1. Where the tenant was obliged by the terms of the tenancy to make the improvement.
2. To the extent that the landlord has made an allowance or benefit in consideration of it.
3. To the extent that the landlord has paid compensation for it.

The arbitrator disregards the tenant's occupation of the holding and any dilapidation or deterioration or damage caused or permitted by the tenant.

There is nothing about comparables or scarcity.

It is not possible to contract out of the rent review procedure unless a formula has been adopted or the rent is stated to remain fixed (s 9).

Compensation on termination

Sections 15–27 of the 1995 Act provide for compensation on the termination of the tenancy in respect of tenant's improvements.

A tenant's improvement is defined by *section 15* as:

Any physical improvement which is made on the holding by the tenant by his own effort or wholly or partly at his own expense or

Any intangible advantage which is obtained for the holding by the tenant by his own effort or wholly or partly at his own expense and becomes attached to the holding.

An example of the latter would be a quota which remained attached to the holding. There are also express provisions relating to unoperated planning permissions.

Section 16 provides the basic entitlement to compensation. Compensation not surprisingly is not paid for any physical improvement which is removed from the holding or any intangible advantage which does not remain attached to the holding.

Statutory compensation for milk quota does not apply (s 16(3)).

No compensation is payable unless either the landlord consented to the improvement under sections 17 or 18 or an arbitrator consented on the landlord's behalf to the improvement under section 19.

The landlord's consent may be given in the tenancy agreement or elsewhere and may be given either unconditionally or on condition that the tenant agrees to a specified variation in the terms of the tenancy. It does not appear that the usual writing down condition would be appropriate given that it is not possible to contract out of the provisions in the Act for computation of the compensation (see s 26).

Section 18 refers to planning permission expressly.

The landlord has to consent both to the application for planning permission (s 18(1)(a)) and to the specific physical improvement or change of use the subject of the planning application (s 18(1)(b)).

Furthermore compensation is only payable for the planning permission in the event that the improvement has not been completed or the change of use effected by the termination of the tenancy.

No consent may be given to an improvement which has been provided or begun to be provided except a routine improvement (s 19(2)). Routine improvement is defined in section 19(10) as a physical improvement made in the normal course of farming not being fixed equipment *i.e.* tenantright. It does not include any improvement prohibited by the terms of the tenancy. Fixed equipment is clarified in section 19(10) as, *inter alia*, anything grown for a purpose other than:

- use after severance
- consumption of the thing grown or its produce
- amenity.

Accordingly routine improvements can include quite long term improvements *e.g.* tree planting.

Section 19 does not apply to a planning application under section 18 and so the landlord can refuse to consent to this if he wishes. Section 19(1)(a) only refers to a refusal under section 17(1).

If the landlord fails to give consent within two months of a written request or makes a condition which the tenant regards as unreasonable he may give notice in writing to the landlord requiring that the question should be referred to arbitration (s 19(1)).

There is a time limit on the tenant serving that notice. He must serve it within two months after the refusal or the conditional consent was given. If the landlord simply does nothing he must serve notice within four months of the request *i.e.* within two months after the landlord's two months period expires (s 19(2)).

Either the parties can agree on an arbitrator or if not either party can apply to the President of the RICS to appoint one (s 19(3)). There is apparently no time limit during which this appointment has to be made. However, the tenant must not go ahead with the improvement, except a routine improvement, until the process is completed; if he does the application is aborted (s 19(9)).

The arbitrator has to have regard "to the terms of the tenancy and any other relevant circumstances (including the circumstances of the tenant and the landlord)" (s 19(4)).

The arbitrator cannot give approval subject to any condition or vary any condition required by the landlord; he may only give or refuse approval (s 19(6)). Section 19(8) provides that if the arbitrator refuses consent it does not affect the validity of the landlord's consent or of the condition subject to which it was given. Presumably the landlord can withdraw his conditional consent if the tenant applies for arbitration.

Section 20 contains the formula for calculating compensation. It is "an amount equal to the increase attributable to the improvement in the value of the holding at the termination of the tenancy as land comprised in a tenancy". It is not clear how this will be interpreted. It is likely that it will be the capitalised rental value of the improvement calculated by reference to the period within which it is likely to remain useful. There is a useful discussion in CAAV booklet 166, December 1995 "Commentary on the valuation of improvements under the ATA 1995".

Any contribution by the landlord is to be taken into account provided it is covered by an agreement in writing and any grant aid is also to be taken into account by reference to the proportion of the benefit or grant to the total cost (s 20(2) and (3)).

Although no compensation is payable for an executed planning permission if the fact of that planning permission increases the value of the physical improvement that increase would be taken into account.

Clearly the tenant will need a written consent to provide his entitlement to compensation. The landlord will need one if he is to contribute to the cost of the improvement and have his contribution taken into account.

Section 21 provides for the amount of compensation for planning permission. The compensation is "an amount equal to the increase attributable to the fact that the relevant development is authorised by the planning permission in the value of the holding at the termination of the tenancy as land comprised in a tenancy". Once again there is a reduction for any benefit provided by the landlord provided it is documented.

Section 22 contains the provision for making the claim for compensation. The tenant has to serve notice within two months after the end of the tenancy in writing of his intention to make the claim and of the nature of the claim (s 22(2)). The landlord and the tenant can settle the claim by agreement or can agree on the appointment of an arbitrator. If neither of these happens then either party may after the end of the period of four months beginning with the date of termination of the tenancy apply to the President of the RICS to appoint an arbitrator. Once again there appears to be no long stop time limit on this.

In the case of a routine improvement there is provision for the application for consent and compensation to be consolidated and only one fee paid (s 22(4)).

Section 23 governs the position under successive tenancies.

Section 24 considers the situation where there is notice to quit part. If the improvement is on that part compensation is calculated by reference to the whole holding.

Section 25 provides for compensation where the reversionary interest is severed with a view not to disadvantage the tenant.

Section 26 prevents contracting out. Section 26(2) confirms that the tenant can still obtain compensation for other matters. This means it is open to the parties to agree on compensation for disturbance, dilapidations and any other matters not specifically covered in the Act.

Arbitration

Section 28 makes provision for arbitration of any disputes arising other than those as to rent review refusal of consent to a tenant's improvement or the compensation provisions in respect of tenant's improvements.

Either party may give notice in writing to the other specifying the dispute and stating that unless before the end of the period of two months beginning with the day on which the notice is given the parties have appointed an arbitrator by agreement he proposes to apply to the President of the RICS for the appointment of an arbitrator by him. Either party may apply to the President if no arbitrator has been appointed by agreement within the two month period. There does not appear to be a time limit for such an appointment.

Section 29 encourages ADR. The arbitration provision does not apply if:

- The tenancy agreement includes provision for disputes to be resolved by a person other than:
  - the landlord or the tenant; or
  - a third party appointed by either of them without the consent or concurrence of the other and; either
    - (i) the landlord and the tenant have jointly referred the dispute to the third party under the provision; or
    - (ii) the landlord or the tenant has referred the dispute to the third party and notified the other in writing of the making of the reference, the period of four weeks beginning with the date on which the other was so notified has expired, and the other has not given an arbitration notice under section 28(2).

It appears therefore that if there is machinery in the agreement and one party receives a notice he has four weeks within which to apply for arbitration if he wants to do so.

A sole arbitrator is to determine the matter (s 30).

There are various miscellaneous items which are not covered here as being of relatively restricted interest.

Mortgagors

Section 31 relates to a mortgagor's power of leasing and amends section 99 of the Law of Property Act 1925. Effectively nothing in a mortgage deed executed after 1 September 1995 can prevent a 1986 Act tenancy under the succession provisions being granted; otherwise a ban on letting will be effective; in other words a farm business tenancy will be voidable by the mortgagee where there is a ban on letting in the mortgage and the letting is subsequently created. Where a 1986 Act tenancy subsists lenders will need to take care subject to the decision in *AMC* v *Woodward* (1995) 04 EG 143 referred to later.

Documentation

Section 35 alters the Solicitors Act 1974. Documents relating to farm business tenancies (or arrangements reasonably believed to be farm business tenancies) can be drawn by:

- a full member of the CAAV
- an Associate or Fellow of the ISVA
- an Associate or Fellow of the RICS.

This was formerly the prerogative only of Solicitors in respect of leases for more than three years.

Notices

Section 36 relates to the service of notices. Notices can be:

- delivered
- left at the appropriate address
- given in any manner authorised by agreement between the parties.

Fax or other electronic means is expressly excluded unless authorised by agreement (s 36(3)).

The definition of agriculture in the 1986 Act is repeated for the purposes of this Act (s 38(1)).

Farm Business Tenancies of less than five years duration (including periodic tenancies) are disregarded when looking at the commercial unit test for succession purposes (amendment to the 1986 Act in the Schedule).

Possible matters for inclusion in a farm business tenancy agreement

Farm business tenancy agreements are likely to be a combination of current commercial agreements and current agricultural agreements. The important thing to be aware of is those matters in respect of which contracting out is not permitted and those matters which had previously been regulated by the 1986 Act where there will no longer be any supporting machinery.

The terms should include:

- Description of the parties.
- Description of the property.
- The rental. Here it is necessary to consider whether there is to be any review date or machinery for increase or if the rent is to be fixed. If it is to be fixed this must be stated. A formula may be appropriate.
- The term. This will be particularly important. For a term of two years or less there is no extension under the Act. For a term of more than two years the tenancy will continue from year to year unless terminated by 12 months' notice before the end of the term. Where a longer term agreement is considered it is likely to be important to include break clauses for example in the event of death, or nonpayment of rent. The circumstances should be carefully considered. If notice to quit part is required an express provision should be included. Twelve months' notice will be required on a notice to quit part or to operate a break clause.
- Exceptions reservations and rights should be specified where necessary.
- All the usual tenant's covenants will still be inserted. In particular it may be appropriate to consider whether any alterations should be banned. This might be a way of protecting the landlord's

position on tenant's improvements to some extent. A restriction on user to "agriculture" may be considered if the agricultural condition is in point: see section 1(8). A restriction on cropping and amenity planting may be desirable. This may affect rental and also possible liability for tenant's improvements under section 19. If the tenant covenants to comply with statutory requirements he should consider how onerous these are likely to be especially with the increased emphasis on environmental matters now experienced.

– Repairing and insurance obligations will have to be spelt out since the model clauses will no longer be applicable.
– Landlord's covenant for quiet enjoyment.
– Dilapidations. As there are no statutory dilapidations provisions these will have to be included in the agreement.
– CAP. All the CAP implications will need to be considered. Express clauses will be required to cover milk quota, livestock premium rights and arable aid payments (as appropriate).

Points which might be appropriate to consider are:

– Restriction on voluntary setaside.
– Provision of information.
– Obligation to maintain quotas especially where the holding has milk quota attached.
– Provisions to enable the tenant to deal with his own quota (especially milk quota). He may need the right to sublet to move the quota but the subletting should expire before the tenancy ends. Possibly the landlord may want a pre-emption opportunity.
– Provisions for arable aid and setaside payments. It may be easiest to provide for any aid payable after the tenancy ends to go to the landlord subject to compensating the tenant. The landlord may want to make a retention out of any payments due to the tenant pending receipt of the aid.
– Obligations on both parties to comply with the IACS requirements.
– Holdover. The tenant may wish to harvest crops in the ground rather than claim compensation for routine improvements.
– Forfeiture clause. Although the Law Commission has suggested that forfeiture be abolished, until it is, a wide ranging forfeiture clause should be inserted. This is the only clause which will be available to recover possession on less than 12 months notice for longer tenancies. Having regard to *Parry* v *Million Pigs Ltd* (1980) 260 EG 281 it is necessary to make sure that the notice period is long enough to permit the tenant to protect his position. The right to remove fixtures may be in point.

It may be worth mentioning one or two general points on farm business tenancies.

- It is essential to consider from a fiscal point of view whether or not a Farm Business Tenancy is what is required. Although the inheritance tax position has been alleviated there are still potential problems with income tax and capital gains tax which ought to be considered.
- Although the risk of security of tenure has disappeared the Revenue may seek to set up a tenancy arrangement rather than some other arrangement if it is to the Revenue's advantage to do so.
- As the short notice provisions are not available forfeiture will be very important.
- As the model clauses are not available permissive and voluntary waste and other obscure areas of law may become relevant.
- Several landlords are approaching their tenants with a view to negotiating surrenders and regrants. Clearly tenants must be very wary in view of the very different system and rent level and the terms must be carefully considered.
- A surrender and regrant can arise unexpectedly. For example, an extension of the term or an addition of further land may effect this. It is imperative to be aware of the risks in view of the restrictive terms of section 4(1)(f) (considered in more detail above).

CHAPTER 7

General Points on Notices

The Agricultural Holdings legislation contains many sections which require the service of notices within strict time limits. It is essential that great care is taken with this since it is all too easy to fail to serve a notice properly or to miss a time limit. Section 93 of the 1986 Act and section 36 of the 1995 Act are the relevant sections.

Where proof of service is vital personal service will be the safest route.

In *Lord Newborough* v *Jones* [1974] 3 All ER 17 service by Recorded Delivery failed. The landlord went to the tenant's house and knocked on the door. Receiving no answer and as there was no letter box he pushed the notice under the door. The tenant said it slid under the linoleum and was not found for six months. It was held that it was good service. Service was also considered in *Datnow* v *Jones* (1985) 2 EGLR 1. There, service at the farmhouse by one person deemed honest was good service. However, corroboration may be safer.

Where time limits apply then the timing is absolutely crucial. An example is the *Luttenberger* case.

More than one tenant

Where there is more than one tenant, at common law a notice addressed to all the tenants and served on one is good. It is however safer to serve on all the tenants and statute may require that. In *Jones* v *Lewis* (1973) 226 EG 805 notice was addressed to and served on one of two joint tenants. It was held that service was bad.

There is nothing to stop a landlord serving notice to quit although the landlord himself is one of the tenants. See *Brenner* v *Rose* [1973] 2 All ER 535.

Normally all the tenants must join in serving a counter notice. However, in the case of *Featherstone* v *Staples* [1986] 2 All ER 461 the court held that where the landlord or his nominee was one of the tenants the other tenants alone could serve the appropriate counter notice. This was despite an express provision to the contrary in the partnership agreement which the Court of Appeal regarded as contrary to public policy and therefore unenforceable.

In *Cork* v *Cork* (1997) EG 130 an injunction was granted on an interlocutory basis to compel an absentee joint tenant to join in serving a counter notice. His co-tenant undertook to surrender or otherwise determine the tenancy if ultimately it was found that he should not have been compelled to join in the counter notice.

Under the general law one tenant can normally serve notice to quit but by analogy with *Featherstone* v *Staples* where the landlord is one of the tenants it is probably unlikely that a notice to quit served by the landlord or his nominee in his capacity as tenant would be upheld.

In any case where landlord and tenant are joint tenants together it is likely that there will be a trust imposed restricting either of the tenants from taking action which would be adverse to the interests of both of them as tenants. Where there are partners and the partnership ceases careful consideration must be given to the consequences in respect of the value of any partnership tenancy and milk quota.

Harrow London Borough Council v Johnstone (1995) EGCS 53

Husband and wife were joint tenants of a Council flat. They fell out and the husband obtained an injunction preventing the wife excluding him from the property. The wife was required by the Council to serve notice to quit before she was rehoused. The husband claimed that the notice to quit was in breach of the injunction. The Court of Appeal (by a majority) held that the wife and the Council were in contempt of court and the notice to quit could not be relied on by them so long as the injunction was extant. On appeal the decision was reversed by the House of Lords because the injunction did not require the wife to co-operate in preserving the tenancy and the Council had no knowledge of the matrimonial proceedings. One can see that this case could apply in an agricultural context.

More than one landlord

Where the reversion has been severed statute assists with the service of a notice to quit (s140LPA 1925). However there is no similar provision regarding rent review in either the 1986 Act or the 1995 Act. Either the holdings should be expressly split (if the tenant will agree) or appropriate documentation should be entered into obliging all the landlords to join in such a notice. The tenant would normally be ill-advised to agree to a split as he could find he has two farm business tenancies instead of one 1986 Act tenancy. In the case of a farm business tenancy the landlord can, if the agreement allows, terminate the tenancy and start again. Section 11 of the 1995 Act makes provision to protect the tenant from a premature review in such a case.

A notice to quit given by one or some of the landlords where a property is owned jointly is good: see *Parsons* v *Parsons* (1983) 269 EG 634.

It is possible to serve too many notices! A case on the 1986 Act where this occured is:

Lower v Sorrell [1962] 3 All ER 1074
The landlord served a valid notice to quit. One day before it expired another notice to quit a year later was served. The Court of Appeal held that the second notice was ineffective because served before the commencement of the tenancy. Rent was accepted however during the supposed term of the second notice. This created a new tenancy which was protected.

Wording of notices

In *Crawford* v *Elliott* (1991) 13 EG 163 the wording required in a notice to quit was considered. Provided it was clear it was valid.

A similar case is *Walker* v *Crocker* (1992) 23 EG 123. There a letter was sent saying "if your clients are successful on 20 November then our client expects compensation for all his input into the farm including the value of the (milk) quota". This was held to be good notice under section 83 of the 1986 Act and section 11 and Schedule 1 Agriculture Act 1986.

However, as a matter of caution it is safer to follow the precedents.

Fraudulent notices

Rous v Mitchell [1991] 1 WLR 469
Notice to quit was served under Case E on the ground of unlawful subletting. The landlord had forgotten permitting the tenant to sublet cottages. It was held that a statement in a document made recklessly was fraudulent and a fraudulent notice was invalid.

Omivale Limited v Bolden (1994) EGCS 63 CA
This case was decided the other way. The landlord obtained planning permission for conversion of farm buildings for residential purposes. A

notice to quit was served including not only the property the subject of the planning permission but also some extra "amenity land". Although the court accepted that the notice included a larger area and the persons who served it knew of that, they held by a majority that it did not constitute fraud.

It is interesting, however, that the tenant would probably have won had he sought arbitration on the notice.

It is clearly desirable to ensure that both the plans on the planning application and on the notice to quit are the same and all the "amenity" land should be included in the application.

Notices on death

Section 18 Law of Property (Miscellaneous Provisions) Act 1994 changes the procedure for serving notice in the event of a person's death. The notice should be addressed to "the Personal Representatives of" the deceased naming him and left at or sent by post to his last known place of residence or business in the United Kingdom and a copy of it similarly addressed served on the Public Trustee. There is provision under the Public Trustee (Notices Affecting Land) (Title on Death) Regulations 1995 SI 1995 No 1330 providing for registration of such notices, the form to be sent and public access to the Register. The appropriate fee must be paid.

CHAPTER 8

Forfeiture

Nothing in the 1986 Act or the 1995 Act affects the landlord's right to forfeit the tenancy in an appropriate case. Under the 1995 Act forfeiture may be the only way to recover possession timeously. However sometimes forfeiture clauses are invalid following the case of *Parry* v *Million Pigs Ltd* (1980) 260 EG 281. Prior to forfeiture the tenant must have time to serve notice on the landlord to secure compensation rights. Most properly drawn forfeiture clauses where the 1986 Act applies provide for six weeks notice. It remains to be seen what is an appropriate period under the 1995 Act. Possibly the tenant needs time to consider removing his fixtures. Two months would probably be appropriate.

It may be possible to forfeit the tenancy if the appointment of a receiver is included in the forfeiture clause.

Forfeiture is available in some circumstances under a 1986 Act tenancy where the notice to quit procedure is not. However the court can order relief against forfeiture and so it may be less certain of success.

CHAPTER 9

Ineffective Arrangements Sham and Section 423 Insolvency Act 1986

There was a great temptation to enter into arrangements designed to avoid the effects of the 1986 Act. Some of these were artificial in the extreme and in any event were not operated by the parties in accordance with their terms. Even after the 1995 Act it may still be important particularly for fiscal reasons in some cases to ensure that arrangements made do not constitute a tenancy. Examples are:

- to obtain Inheritance Tax relief at 100% after two years occupation rather than seven years ownership;
- for capital gains tax rollover or retirement relief.

The arrangements made can be attacked as shams if they are not what they appear to be.

The principles were enunciated in *Street* v *Mountford* (a residential case) [1985] 2 All ER 289. As Lord Templeman put it "The manufacture of a five pronged implement for manual digging results in a fork even if the manufacturer, unfamiliar with the English language, insists that he intended to make and has made a spade". Examples in an agricultural context have already been mentioned; for example, *Short Bros (Plant) Ltd* v *Edwards* and *Gisborne* v *Burton*.

To avoid these problems it is necessary to ensure that the arrangements made are what they purport to be. For example if a Contracting Agreement in fact transfers occupation of the farm it is highly likely to create a tenancy.

It is important to make sure that the parties understand the arrangements referred to in the document and that they are able and willing to operate them properly.

Arrangements made with a view to defrauding creditors may also be set aside under section 423 Insolvency Act 1986. Examples are:

Midland Bank Plc v Wyatt & Others (1994) EGCS 113 Ch
A declaration of trust by Wyatt that he held property on trust for his wife and daughters was set aside both as a sham and under section 423 Insolvency Act 1986.

AMC Plc v Woodward & Woodward (1995) 04 EG 143
A letting by husband to wife for full rental was set aside on the grounds that it was a "transaction at an undervalue".

PART 2

The Common Agricultural Policy

Introduction

This part of the book considers the legal aspects of the Common Agricultural Policy which are of most relevance to farmers and landowners and their advisers. After an initial introduction the various schemes imposing quotas and providing subsidies are considered. Finally the Integrated Administration and Control System and compensatory schemes are discussed.

It is not intended to describe how the schemes work – the literature published by the Ministry of Agriculture Fisheries and Food does this adequately. It is intended to highlight potential problems and opportunities of which farmers and landowners and their advisers should be aware.

For the advisers, the notes on timing in Appendix 7 should help to put in perspective the requirements of the various schemes. It is necessary to be aware of them in dealing with land transactions including family rearrangements and the administration of estates.

European Regulations

By reason of the United Kingdom's membership of the European Union, European Regulations have direct effect in the United Kingdom. There are two types, Council Regulations and Commission Regulations. In general the Council Regulations are the principal Regulations and the Commission Regulations are more detailed. They are published in the *Official Journal*. The principal Regulations affecting the schemes considered in this Part of the book are reproduced in the Appendices.

Because these Regulations are effective directly in the United Kingdom it is necessary to be aware of them and if a problem arises to refer back to them. Some of the Rules are incorporated in United Kingdom law by Statutory Instrument made under the authority of the European Communities Act 1972 for example the Dairy Produce Quotas Regulations. In other cases the European Regulations are given direct effect by arrangements made by the Ministry.

If anybody is dissatisfied with the UK's implementation of Regulations, the usual remedy is judicial review. The crucial point is that action must be taken promptly *i.e.* within three months in the absence of special circumstances.

Examples in this context are: *R* v *Dairy Produce Quota Tribunal for England and Wales, ex parte Casswell* [1989] 1WLR 1089 where an application made after two years was refused.

Hood v *NFU* (1994) 01 EG 109. The NFU were advising Mr & Mrs Hood regarding the allocation of milk quota. They failed to advise them to challenge the Dairy Produce Quota Tribunal allocation by judicial review within three months. It was held that the NFU were liable because they held themselves out as competent to advise, knowing that the farmers would rely on their advice.

R v *MAFF ex parte NFU*, QBD [1995] 3 CMLR 116. The Court upheld a challenge to the UK rules on awarding suckler cow and sheep quota to developers (notwithstanding that some claims were out of time). The UK had provided that written evidence of development plans prior to 1 January 1993 was required. The Court felt this was unduly restrictive of MAFF's discretion and the rules would have to be altered. New rules were issued, namely the Sheep Annual Premium and Suckler Cow Premium Quotas (Reassessment of Eligibility) Regulations 1996, SI 1996 No 48.

R v *MAFF ex parte Country Landowners' Association* [1996] 2 CMLR 193. The CLA applied for judicial review of the rules relating to livestock premium rights so far as they affected landowners. The Association argued that it was unfair that tenants could remove their quota from tenanted holdings. The Queen's Bench Division referred various questions to the European Court. The European Court of Justice delivered an opinion adverse to the CLA and the case was abandoned.

However, just because the outcome appears unfair, there is not necessarily a legal remedy *Stubbs* v *Hunt & Wrigley & Another* (1992) 20 EG 107 was a case in point. Mr Stubbs changed his farming arrangements in 1984, one consequence being that he was not awarded any milk quota. His application on the grounds of hardship was rejected as he did not fall within any of the specified grounds. The NFU advised that judicial review would not succeed. Mr Stubbs sued his solicitors and the NFU for negligence. The case against the solicitors was abandoned and the Court held the NFU's advice had been correct and, therefore, his claim failed.

The UK courts may well refer a case to the European Court. An example of this is *R* v *MAFF, ex parte D C Bostock* [1994] 3 CMLR 547 relating to compensation for milk quota for a tenant giving up possession of his holding prior to 1986.

CHAPTER 10

Milk Quota

General comment

The intention of the quotas is to limit over production of milk. This is achieved by imposing a levy on producers in the event of the country concerned producing too much milk. In other words a producer will not necessarily be liable to a levy if he produces more than his quota unless the country as a whole is over quota. This is further divided between purchasers (the dairies or Milk Marque) in the case of wholesale quota so that liability may also depend on what other suppliers to that purchaser have done.

The quotas are managed by the Intervention Board.

Quota is registered in the name of the producer. Usually the quota concerned is wholesale quota although occasionally it is direct sales quota (where the producer sells direct).

The producer receives a monthly statement showing the milk produced and comparing it with quota so that the producer can monitor his production.

An extract from the principal Council Regulation is reproduced in Appendix 1. The rules are given effect in the United Kingdom by the Dairy Produce Quotas Regulations 1997, SI 1997 No 733 amended by SI 1997 No 1093. The Agriculture Act 1986 makes provision for rent review and compensation on termination of certain tenancies.

By Regulation 32 there is provision for confiscation of unused quota, although it can be recovered within six years.

Sale and purchase of quota

Until 1994 quota could only be transferred with land. This meant that the seller of quota would let an area of land to the buyer either for grazing or mowing or on a *Gladstone* v *Bower* agreement. The buyer would undertake not to use the land for milk production. The parties would agree the quantity of quota apportioned to the land. That apportionment was supposed to be on the basis of areas of land used for milk production and the Ministry said that they would investigate sample transactions. They gave some helpful guidance that they would not regard more than 20,000 litres per hectare as a reasonable apportionment. While the tenancy subsisted the area let would form part of the purchaser's holding. At the end of the tenancy the quota remained with the purchaser because he had not used that particular area of land for milk production and therefore no quota attached to it. As the apportionment can be questioned later a clause is required providing for compensation in the event of more or less quota than expected being transferred. There was always some doubt as to the efficacy of this procedure but it has usually worked perfectly well in practice.

It was important that occupation should change and therefore there was often a supporting contracting arrangement preferably with a third party but often with the vendor of the quota who would do the work on the land on behalf of the purchaser. The consequence of completing the documentation but not transferring occupation was considered in the case of *R* v *Ministry of Agriculture and Fisheries, ex parte Cox* (1993) 22 EG 111. There Mrs Cox purchased milk quota and took a grazing licence of part of the farm. In fact she never occupied the land and the vendor took occupation of it part way through the licence. The vendor subsequently claimed the quota on the ground that occupation had not been transferred. An arbitrator found that the quota had not been transferred. The Ministry therefore proposed to correct the register by deducting the quota transferred from Mrs Cox's holding. The judge confirmed that occupation had to take place to transfer the quota. However, as the Ministry had declined to alter the registration two years after the transfer the court was not prepared to reopen the matter seven years later. Fortunately for the purchaser therefore she was able to retain the quota.

This method of transfer of quota using a short farm business tenancy for more than ten months is still available and is likely to be the norm. If the apportionment is not made accurately on the basis of areas used for milk production the parties should be warned of the risks, especially in the event of the insolvency of one of them. Any arrangements made must be done properly and carried into effect.

Regulation 11 provides an opportunity to transfer quota without land. If this regulation is followed the Intervention Board has to be satisfied that the transfer is necessary for the development of both parties' businesses. There are also restrictions on the acquisition of further quota by the transferor and the disposal of the quota by the transferee before the expiration of the quota year following the transfer. This has led to a "two tier" market; although the risks are clearly eliminated.

Disposal of part of the holding

Where any part of the holding of a dairy farmer is disposed of, if that part was used for dairy production then quota will pass automatically whatever the parties say. It is therefore imperative to make provision for this in the sale contract. If no quota is intended to pass then it must be stated that this is so and that should any pass despite the terms of the contract the acquirer will compensate the vendor.

The apportionment of quota on the disposal of part of a holding was considered in *Puncknowle Farms v Kane* [1985] 3 All ER 790. It attaches to all parts of the holding used for dairy cows, bulls and followers including areas where corn is grown for feeding to them and possibly where straw is grown for bedding purposes. It is apportioned on an arithmetical basis *i.e.* across the acreage rather than by reference to the fixed equipment as well.

Posthumus v Oosterwoud [1992] 2 CMLR 336
This was a Dutch case where a tenancy of part of a holding terminated. The European Court held that the apportionment should be on a strict acreage basis in the absence of any other objective criteria having been adopted.

Transfer within a quota holder's holding

Where a producer occupies more than one holding he is in a position to massage quota from one holding to another by varying the areas used for milk production. This can adversely affect a landlord and an appropriate restriction should be included in new tenancy agreements.

Holdcroft v Staffordshire County Council (1994) 28 EG 131
This was a case where the Court of Appeal had to consider what appears to have been a failed attempt to massage quota from one holding to another.

The facts were rather complicated.

- 20 March 1989, Mr Holdcroft (tenant) gave notice to the Council to terminate the tenancy of Lower Moddershall Farm. He farmed in partnership with his wife and son. The partners were registered with quota of 190, 373 litres.
- 27 February 1990, the son and daughter-in-law purchased Holly Bank Farm without quota.
- February 1990, the MMB was informed of the purchase of the new farm and that milk production would be moved to the new farm.
- 1 March 1990, the father and his wife retired from the partnership and the son's wife joined. The dairy herd was moved to Holly Barn Farm.

- 2 March 1990, Mr Holdcroft senior farmed Lower Moddershall Farm on his own.
- 25 March 1990, Mr Holdcroft vacated most of Lower Moddershall Farm a further part being vacated later.

There were, therefore, the following transfers of occupation of Lower Moddershall Farm :

1 March 1990 – to the new partners
2 March 1990 – to the father
25 March 1990 – to the Council

The arbitrator awarded 42 litres of the quota to Holly Bank Farm and 190,331 litres to Lower Moddershall Farm.

Moving from one holding to another

Holdcroft illustrates the potential risks of moving from one dairy farm to another. Strictly it appears that the following is required:

- The vendor retains occupation of the former holding for 5 years as well as the new holding but does not use the old holding for milk production. The quota will then have been massaged. This is unlikely to be attractive to a purchaser of the old holding.
- The vendor farms the new holding as a different producer and takes a tenancy of the old holding for more than 10 months in the new name. The old holding is not used for milk production in this period. Effectively the transfer procedure is followed. Even this may be unattractive especially if the old holding is farmed as a dairy farm.
- The vendor sells the old holding with quota and buys a new holding and quota.

It is thought that vendors tend to ignore this in practice. The risk should be pointed out and compensation clauses inserted in the contract but if practicable the transaction should be done properly.

Landlord and tenant

Tenancies created before 2 April 1984 and replacements of them
Tenancies created before 2 April 1984 and renewals of or successions to those tenancies are covered by the provisions of section 13 and Schedule 1 Agriculture Act 1986.

When a tenancy ends the quota will transfer with the land to the landlord or the incomer (because of the change of occupation which occurs). The 1986 Act makes provision for the payment of compensation to the tenant. The detailed rules set out in Schedule 1 are very complicated. The calculation is as follows:

1. Ascertain the "relevant quota". Where the tenant occupies only one holding this will be all of his quota. Where he occupies more than one holding the quota is apportioned in accordance with the *Puncknowle Farms* and *Posthumus* cases.

2. Take out any quota transferred onto the holding at the tenant's expense – he will be compensated for this "transferred quota". The balance is "allocated quota".

3. Work out the "standard quota". To do this one first ascertains the "relevant number of hectares" *i.e.* the average number of hectares of the holding used during the relevant period for the feeding of dairy cows on the land or which might have been expected to be used for that purpose. The relevant period in most cases is 1 January 1983 to 31 December 1983 and so evidence must be retained to support the claim. The test is narrower than the *Puncknowle Farms* test. One multiplies the relevant number of hectares by the prescribed quota per hectare. This is set out by statutory instrument, the Milk Quota (Calculation of Standard Quota) Order, as amended from time to time.

However, there is a potential adjustment to the prescribed quota per hectare. By paragraph 6 (2) of the Schedule where by virtue of the quality of the land or climatic conditions the amount of milk which would reasonably have been expected to have been produced from one hectare of the land during the relevant period ("the reasonable amount") is greater or less than the prescribed average yield per hectare (set out in the statutory instrument) the prescribed quota per hectare is altered. The alternative is achieved by adjusting the prescribed quota proportionally to the reasonable amount and the prescribed average yield.

This was considered in *Grounds* v *Attorney General of the Duchy of Lancaster and Another* (1989) 21 EG 73. There it was held by the Court of Appeal that in working out the reasonable amount the arbitrator should assume that the cattle were fed (inter alia) on such concentrates as a reasonably skilful and successful farmer would use.

In *Surrey County Council* v *Main* (1992) 06 EG 159 the County Court considered the same paragraph. In that case the arbitrator had taken the view that the farm was a normal one to which paragraph 6(1) (the usual case) and not paragraph 6(2) applied. The landlords argued that in every case the paragraph 6(2) computation should be undertaken. It was held that the arbitrator was right.

If the allocated quota is more than the standard quota the tenant is compensated for this excess quota.

4. Work out the "tenant's fraction" of the standard quota. This is calculated as:

Annual rental value of tenant's dairy improvements
and fixed equipment in the relevant period (input rental)
input rental + rental in the relevant period of land then used
for feeding accommodation or milking of dairy cows on the land

The tenant is compensated for the tenant's fraction. Once again the records have to be kept to establish the tenant's fraction.

This was considered in *Creear* v *Fearon* (1994) 46 EG 202. There the Court of Appeal held that if the rent during the relevant period is artificially low and therefore the tenant's fraction is artificially high no adjustment is to be made.

The tenant is compensated for the value of the quota on termination of the tenancy. This will not necessarily be the same as the sale price of quota in the open market. The problem of valuation was considered in the County Court case of *Carson* v *Cornwall County Council* (1993) 03 EG 119. Three possible methods had been considered:

1. The price paid for quota on purchase using a short term letting to transfer quota from one producer to another.
2. A sum calculated by capitalising annual lease payments for quota.
3. A comparison of land sales with vacant possession with and without quota.

It was held that the arbitrator's choice of Method 2 was correct as most nearly achieving the objective of compensating the tenant for "the setting up of milk production on the holding" by him.

There is provision for agreement or arbitration to take place on the standard quota and tenant's fraction before the end of the tenancy. Some landlords are doing this, presumably fearing that as time goes by the necessary evidence needed to work out the calculation will disappear.

There may be a problem where the quota is not registered in the name of the tenant perhaps because he farms through a company. In this case probably the best that can be done is to complete a declaration of trust that the quota belongs to the tenant. The position has not yet been litigated.

If a tenant intends to buy in quota he ought to try and persuade his landlord to agree to co-operate in the event of him wishing to sell it again. Otherwise he may be unable to sell it later if necessary.

Section 15 Agriculture Act 1986 makes provision for transferred quota on rent arbitration.

Tenants who vacated their holdings before the Agriculture Act 1986 came into force on 25 September 1986 are not entitled to compenstion for the loss of their quota; *R* v *MAFF, ex parte DC Bostock* [1994] 3 CMLR 547.

Other tenancies

In granting new tenancies milk quota must be borne in mind.

If there is quota attached to the holding it will pass to the tenant as the new occupier. It will revert to the landlord when the tenant vacates without compensation. The landlord should make provision to prevent the tenant massaging the quota and to provide for compensation if he does so.

If the tenant brings quota to the holding he will require a clause enabling him to remove it before the end of the tenancy. He should oblige the landlord to sign the necessary forms and permit a subletting (expiring before the tenancy ends) and provide for compensation if the quota passes in error. Any quota he leaves will be treated as an improvement subject to the terms of the 1995 Act *i.e.* if consent was obtained compensation would be payable. However the compensation obtained is unlikely to be the same as the "value" of the quota on a sale.

Leasing

Leasing of quota is also possible and appears to cause little problem in practice. One point to watch is that it is virtually impossible to be certain that the lessor has quota to let. If he does not, it may be too late to lease replacement quota by the time the problem is revealed (leasing stops on 31 December).

Ownership of quota

Although quota is registered in the name of the producer it will not necessarily belong to the producer. Examples of this are *Faulks v Faulks*

(1992) 15 EG 82 where the quota although registered in the name of a partnership was held to belong to the surviving partner with the tenancy of the land. *Davies* v *H & R Ecroyd Ltd* (1996) EGCS 77 where a freehold farm was made available for use by partners. The quota was held to belong to the freeholder.

SLOM producers

Some producers who joined the various schemes for reducing production prior to the introduction of milk quotas claimed that they were unfairly treated. These are called SLOM producers and arrangements have been made to provide quota for them.

A case where the Ministry awarded SLOM II quota and subsequently withdrew it is *R* v *MAFF, ex parte St Clere's Hall Farm and others* (1995) EGCS 75. The Ministry argued that the partnership arrangements made by the farmers were insufficient to constitute the resumption of production within the scheme.

There are restrictions on disposal of SLOM quota in certain cases until December 1996 and if those restrictions are not complied with the quota will revert to the national reserve.

Cross border producers

It was confirmed by the European Court of Justice in *Katholische Kirchengemeinde St Martinus Elten* v *Landwirtschaftskammer Rheinland* Case C 463/93 reported in Proceedings of Court of Justice and Court of First Instance of the European Communities 3/97 p3 that where milk quota was owned by a producer in two countries it would be apportioned in the usual way. The producer there had a holding in the Netherlands and Germany and sold his milk to a German purchaser.

Taxation implications of milk quota transactions

There has been much discussion as to the nature of quota, which is primarily of importance in assessing the tax position.

The Revenue's view is that quota is a separate capital asset and that compensation for cuts and payment for the quota is chargeable to capital gains tax. It is available for rollover and retirement relief in appropriate cases. As it was created in 1984 however, allocated quota has no base value.

It has been suggested that the quota is an interest in land; if so this would have great capital gains tax advantages as it would give the quota a base value. At the moment the Revenue does not accept this. Chadwick J in the *Faulks* case (1992) 15 EG 82 expressed the view that the Revenue is wrong. A case has been decided in favour of the Revenue before the Special Commissioners (*Cottle* v *Coldicott* (1995) STC (SCD) 239).

Payment on termination of tenancy

The position regarding the payment on termination of a tenancy is not clear. Certainly it would be worth arguing that the payment is compensation and tax free on the basis of *Davis* v *Powell*, 1976 STC 492 and *Drummond* v *Austen Brown*, 1984 STC 321 (compensation for disturbance). However the Revenue is unlikely to agree!

If the land is sold with the quota and the price not apportioned it may well be possible to argue that the quota value is part of the land disposal; this would mean that the indexation loss likely on the land can be used against the "gain" on the quota. This is the action which landlords having contingent rights to acquire quota under the Agriculture Act 1986 should take.

Quota sold without land is VATable. Quota sold with land is usually not.

Milk quota and indeed livestock quotas cause difficulties for lenders. An interesting case is *Huish* v *Ellis and others* (1995) NPC 3. There a receiver appointed by a bank sold the farm. As it was a dairy farm the sale carried the quota although the quota was not charged. It was held that the receiver was not obliged to negotiate with the borrower with a view to selling the land and the quota separately in order to realise a higher price. The situation regarding quota was explored further in *Harries* v *Barclays Bank Plc* (1995) NPC 201. There it was held that a charge of the farm effectively carried the right both to lease and sell (with the farm) the quota as incidental to the charge of the land. The decision was upheld on appeal (1997) EGCS 116.

CHAPTER 11

Beef Special Premium Scheme

Under the Beef Special Premium Scheme producers of beef cattle are entitled to payments in the case of steers twice in the life of each animal and in the case of bulls once. Each producer has a maximum entitlement of 90 head of cattle. For the purpose of this scheme a partnership is a single producer. The principal European Regulations are reproduced in Appendix 2.

The Scheme is governed by the Beef Special Premium Regulations 1996, SI 1996 No 3241.

The Ministry Guidance is extremely helpful. The Scheme Notes and Claim Form obtainable from the Ministry provide useful information on how the scheme works. The Ministry also publishes a useful booklet *CAP Reform in the Beef Sector*.

Normally no points of difficulty arise in respect of this scheme. One point to watch is the retention period in order to ensure that the right to premium is not lost, for example on a change of partnership arrangements. The retention period is two months and runs from the day after the claim is lodged or such later date up to two months from lodgement as the producer chooses and notifies. Forage area is required. The area must be available to the claimant or someone else for grazing or taking a forage crop for at least seven months beginning between 1 January and 31 March. For at least four of these seven months it must be available to the claimant. Any changes in respect of forage area must be carefully timed and if necessary documented to avoid the loss of aid.

CHAPTER 12

Suckler Cow Premium Scheme

This scheme provides for the payment of premium for suckler cows maintained on a holding. The premium is paid annually and subject to a quota. The principal European Regulations governing the scheme are set out in Appendix 3. The scheme is governed by the Suckler Cow Premium Regulations 1993 SI 1993 No 1441 amended by SI 1994 No 1528 SI 1995 No 15, No 1446, SI 1996 No 1488 and SI 1997 No 249. In addition the quotas are governed by the Sheep Annual Premium and Suckler Cow Premium Quotas Regulations 1993 SI 1993 No 1626 amended by SI 1993 No 3036, SI 1994 No 2894, SI 1996 No 48 and 1939.

Once again there is useful guidance issued by the Ministry in the form of The Suckler Cow Premium Scheme Notes for Guidance. There is also a booklet, *Suckler Cow Premium Scheme Quotas*, obtainable from the Ministry.

The claim period runs from 1 July to 31 December. The retention period is six months from the day after the lodgement of the claim. Forage area is required.

Suckler Cow Quotas are transferable.

Quota may be lost if insufficiently used.

The legal points which are likely to arise are as follows:

Transfers of the holding

Unless the quota is transferred with the whole of the producer's holding the siphon of 15% to the National Reserve will operate. The holding is defined as the production unit managed by that producer and is apparently interpreted as including not only suckler cow units but also arable holdings. Therefore if a producer has more than one holding even if the holding with the suckler cows on is being transferred in its entirety together with the quota the siphon may apply. It appears that quota can be transferred even with a short letting. It may be that arrangements such as those used for milk quota transfer will be used.

Family rearrangements

For the purpose of suckler cow quotas a partnership is a single producer. It is however necessary to consider changes within the family on for example a dissolution of partnership especially if the land is not transferred to the same person as the quota. Disposals must be avoided within the retention period. It is not clear if a change of partners would be deemed a disposal. It would be best to time any change on the basis that it might.

Administration of estates

The quota will need to be dealt with in the administration of a deceased person's estate where he is a sole trader. The personal representatives may need to claim the premium during the period of administration. They will need to transfer the quota either on sale or to a beneficiary and notify the Ministry on the appropriate forms. The siphon may apply even on a transfer to a beneficiary if the holding is not also transferred. If this is serious, avoidance for example by a short letting, should be contemplated.

Forage area

Changes to forage area arrangements must be carefully monitored.

CHAPTER 13

Sheep Annual Premium Scheme

Sheep annual premium is payable each year on ewes covered by the scheme. Again the premium payments are subject to quota. The principal European Regulations are set out in Appendix 4.

The scheme is governed by the Sheep Annual Premium Regulations 1992 SI 1992 No 2677 amended by SI 1994 No 2741, SI 1995 No 2779 and SI 1996 No 49.

The quotas are governed by the Sheep Annual Premium and Suckler Cow Premium Quotas Regulations 1993 SI 1993 No 1626 amended by SI 1993 No 3036, SI 1994 No 2894, SI 1996 No 48 and 1939.

The notes for the Scheme are obtainable from the Ministry. In addition the Ministry publishes *Sheep Annual Premium Scheme Quotas Notes for Guidance*.

The claim period is from 4 December to 4 February and the retention period from 5 February to 15 May. Quota may be lost if insufficiently used.

Similar points arise in respect of sheep quota to suckler cow quota in the event of transfers of holdings, retention periods, forage area and the administration of estates. It is more complicated, however, because of the rules relating to producer groups or what we would understand as partnerships. For the sheep scheme each member of a partnership is entitled to his share of quota. This means that the ownership of the sheep and the quota has to coincide. Since the quota is likely to have been awarded on the basis of information supplied by the producer group in connection with the 1991 or 1992 claims it is desirable to ensure that the quota is correctly divided between the partners and that the partnership agreement and accounts fit in with the ownership of the quota.

It may, for example, be necessary if A and B are in partnership to provide for the flock to belong to them in equal shares if they are entitled equally to the quota irrespective of how much capital they may have in the business.

If the shares in the sheep and the quota change during the retention period part of the premium will be lost so it is necessary to ensure that any changes take place on an appropriate date.

If any changes are made to the partnership arrangements then it is essential to consider whether or not the siphon may inadvertently apply. For example if the shares in the sheep are changed but the shares in the underlying holding are not then it appears the siphon will apply.

If a partner owns a sheep farm in partnership and an arable farm on his own account even if the sheep farm and the partnership share change together it is possible that the siphon will apply because the Ministry will regard the arable farm as part of his holding.

There is now a limited exemption from the siphon for transfers between members of producer groups (Reg 2134/95). The transferor and transferee must continue to be members of the group for at least three marketing years following that in respect of which the transfer of rights is notified. The restriction means that the use of the exemption is likely to be severely restricted.

A partner's sheep quota will have to be dealt with individually. The premium rights are freely transferable.

CHAPTER 14

The Arable Scheme

The Arable Area Payment Scheme makes provision for the payment of aid to producers of certain arable crops and for payment of compensation to certain arable producers for setting aside (*i.e.* withdrawing from production) some of their arable land. The principal European Regulations are reproduced in Appendix 5. There are other Regulations for example non-food use of set-aside (Reg 334/93, OJ 1993 L38/12).

The crops concerned are cereals, oilseeds, protein crops and linseed.

The Scheme is governed in the United Kingdom by the Arable Area Payments Regulations 1996 SI 1996 No 3142.

The Ministry Booklets are very helpful. The following are available:

AR7   How to Register your land as eligible for Arable Area Payments

AR8   Five-year Set-aside and the Arable Area Payments Scheme

AR9   Seed Certification and Set-Aside

AR10   Land Transfers

AR11   Installation of Cables and Pipelines

AR12   Compulsory Purchase

AR13   Management of Set-aside Land: Research progress

AR14   How to manage your set-aside land for specific environmental objectives

AR15   Proposed Countryside Access Scheme

AR21   Transferring land from the Five Year Set-aside Scheme to the Arable Area Payments Scheme or the Habitat Scheme

AR23   Base Areas

AR26   Transfers of set-aside obligations between producers

AR28   Explanatory Guide to one to one switches of eligible and ineligible land

AR29   Arable Area Payments (2 volumes)

AR30   Arable Area Payments Scheme 1998 update

The principal area of difficulty is the requirements on a transfer of occupation.

The points to be clarified are:

- That the land is eligible for area aid. This depends usually on the user of the land on 31 December 1991. If possible evidence of acceptance by the Ministry that the land qualifies should be obtained. In two circumstances ineligible land can become eligible:
  - as a replacement for land lost by reason of compulsory purchase using form IACS 17
  - where eligible land is switched for ineligible land for agronomic plant health or environmental reasons using form IACS 21.
- With reference to set-aside, is the land in:
  - obligatory set-aside (5% this year 1997 and next year 1998) by derogation from the norm of 17.5%?
  - guaranteed set-aside available where an undertaking is given to keep the same land set-aside for five years but restricted to land in short rotation coppice and the Countryside Access Scheme?
  - voluntary set-aside (up to 50%)?
  - additional voluntary set-aside (ex five year set-aside land)?
  - transferred set-aside?
  - penalty set-aside?

  It is necessary to consider the implications of a transfer and obtain details of the scheme and any correspondence with the Ministry.
- Is the set-aside land being used for cropping for non-food use? If so, it will be necessary to obtain details of the contract and notifications made.

  Is the set-aside land comprised in a Nitrate Sensitive Area undertaking or the NSA Premium Arable Scheme Set-aside option? If so the detailed arrangements must be clarified.
- Is the set-aside land comprised in the Farm Woodland Premium Scheme or Woodland Grant Scheme? If so the rules of the appropriate scheme must be checked.

  Is the set-aside land comprised in the Habitat Scheme? If so, the rules of that scheme must be checked.
- What acts of cultivation have been carried out to set-aside land during the current set-aside period?
- Have the IACS requirements been complied with? If not what breaches have occurred?
- Who is to apply for aid and who is to receive the payment?
- If the purchaser is to make the claim for aid or receive the payment and, if rape, linseed or sunflower seed is included in the cropping, have the special conditions been met? In particular, the invoices and seed labels will be required. The detailed requirements are referred to in Appendix 5 Part II Arable Area Payments AR29.

Implications of the deal

When a deal is about to be done it is important that both parties understand the implications.

Under the European Regulations the application for aid is to be made by the person who sowed the seed but the Commission has allowed the United Kingdom to provide for the incomer to claim, provided that he is occupying the land at the time the claim is made.

Normally the payments will be made to the person who makes the claim. If this is not acceptable then arrangements will have to be made in the contract for the aid to be paid over by the recipient to the other party.

It is important to remember that the person who makes the claim will be the person who must have the correct proportion of set-aside to arable crops. This will not be affected by the other party's position. It is therefore necessary to decide who should make the claim.

If the set-aside land is being cropped for non-food use then the position is more complicated. If the outgoer is to deliver the crop then no problem arises. If the crop is to be transferred to the incomer then 10 working days notice must be served on MAFF and the Intervention Board before the contract is amended. The contract with the collector or first processor will then have to be assigned.

If the set-aside land is comprised in a Nitrate Sensitive Area undertaking, the NSA Premium Arable Scheme Setaside option, the Farm Woodland Premium Scheme, the Woodland Grant Scheme or the Habitat Scheme, the detailed arrangements made and the rules of the relevant scheme must be checked.

The purchaser must realise the restrictions on set-aside affecting the land if appropriate. He cannot set it aside for two years unless one of the exemptions in Appendix 6 to the Ministry booklet applies. "Normal" set-aside, i.e. 5% this year of a proportion of the holding is now allowed. Apparently the Commission may want this to be altered again so the position should be kept under review. If the purchaser takes possession during the set-aside period he must consult with the Ministry to see if any set-aside will be permitted.

Each party should understand the implications of a breach by either party of the rules of the scheme. In any case where a party is to rely on another person to do or not to do something he must always remember that a warranty that something will be done or not done will only carry a right to damages. That right to damages is only useful to the extent that the warrantor is solvent. There is therefore a degree of risk and it is desirable to minimise as far as possible the reliance of either party on the other. In the light of this it is probably better to try and avoid a change of occupation during the set-aside period. This will be particularly relevant on transfers of setaside.

The sale contract

Certain of these matters should be included in the sale contract. For example:

- Who is to claim the aid and receive the payment?
- A warranty by the vendor as to user on 31 December 1991 and as to areas in set-aside supported by evidence of Ministry acceptance or a statutory declaration. The warranty should extend to any land becoming eligible after 31 December 1991 by the use of forms IACS 17 or IACS 21.
- Where the purchaser is to benefit from the aid in the current year a warranty by the vendor as to the forms submitted under IACS the user of the property that all the requirements of the scheme have been met and will be met up to completion and details of any queries raised by MAFF. If appropriate, copy invoices, seed labels etc should be annexed.
- An agreement by both parties to make available access to the property and all relevant documents to MAFF or their agents.
- An appropriate clause relating to any contract for non-food crops on setaside land, who is to serve notice on MAFF and the Intervention Board and when.
- A clause relating to setaside used for short rotation coppice or included in one of the environmental schemes if appropriate.
- A warranty by the purchaser to comply with the rules of the scheme.
- If necessary a condition obliging any necessary forms under the old or new set-aside scheme or any other relevant scheme or IACS to be completed and filed with MAFF immediately following completion.
- An appropriate tenantright clause dealing if appropriate with an enhancement payment in respect of area aid payable to the purchaser.

Other circumstances

On sales and purchases both parties can be expected to be cooperative. Circumstances may arise where this is not the case.

Insolvency

If a farmer is insolvent then the incoming receiver or trustee must find out immediately what the situation is regarding area aid and take whatever steps he can to ensure its preservation. There may be a problem here if the farmer is insolvent and the land belongs to somebody else so that occupation passes elsewhere within the growing season. Each case will have to be handled on its own particular circumstances.

Existing tenancies

Many existing tenancy agreements will have been framed without considering the implications of IACS. Problems may well arise and the following are examples:

The landlord would no doubt wish to see the tenant's IACS form but would not be entitled to do so unless authorised in the tenancy agreement. The tenant will have to decide whether or not to supply the form in response to the landlord's request. If the landlord is unable to make any progress with the tenant he should ask MAFF if the land has been registered as eligible for area aid and if there is any doubt seek to register it himself. The point of doing this is that it may be harder in years to come to establish user on 31 December 1991.

A tenant would not be in breach of his tenancy agreement in entering into obligatory set-aside as this is essential for the growth of many arable crops. However, entering into the voluntary set-aside scheme may or may not be a breach of the tenancy agreement and the tenant must be careful before doing this.

At the end of the tenancy a transfer of the land will occur either to the landlord or to an incoming tenant. Assuming nothing is agreed regarding area aid if the tenant has made a claim he will be entitled to the aid as the person who has sown the crop. However, his claim may well be affected by activities of the incomer. For example, if the incomer ploughs in the crop of rape or linseed before the flowering stage no aid would be due. It is unlikely that the incomer would have any duty to the outgoer to protect his payment. As part of the tenantright negotiation the outgoer will want to try and ensure that the incomer will do nothing to prevent receipt of compensation.

New tenancies

Clearly with new tenancies consideration should be given to eradicating these points of difficulty. In particular:

The landlord may want to impose an obligation on the tenant to keep him informed about his returns under IACS.

The landlord may also want to restrict the area of the farm to be put into set-aside in each year.

Both parties will wish to ensure that the arrangements on cessation are appropriate, which is likely to mean that they are broadly on the basis of a sale and purchase.

Before granting or taking a tenancy both parties must consider the implications under the CAP arrangements.

Cables and pipelines

The Ministry has considered the problems which may arise with the installation of cables and pipelines. They have issued a booklet AR11 dealing with this. If possession is taken during the growing season the balance cropping and set-aside will be disturbed. It is important to go back to first principles on this and consider the consequences. If possible, works during the set-aside period should be avoided.

CHAPTER 15

Integrated Administration and Control System

The Integrated Administration and Control System is the label under which various of the schemes are administered. In particular, an IACS form giving details of each applicant's holding and cropping has to be submitted by 15 May in each year in order to support applications for arable area payments, beef special premium, suckler cow premium, hill livestock compensatory allowances and sheep annual premium.

Completion of form

The greatest care has to be taken with completion and indeed delivery of the form.

Apart from accuracy, the principal point to consider where there are several possibly connected enterprises is how many forms should be submitted. Convenience in the past has suggested one only, subject to the Ministry accepting this. Should an acreage or financial maximum be imposed on aid payments this would need to be reviewed. As any division of a business simply to obtain extra aid is likely to be ignored the possibility and desirability of restructuring businesses for other purposes should always be borne in mind.

The principal European Regulations are reproduced in Appendix 6.

The Regulations are given effect in the United Kingdom by the Integrated Administration and Control System Regulations 1993, SI 1993 No 1317 amended by SI 1994 No 1134 and SI 1997 No 1148.

The Ministry publishes a useful booklet on the scheme each year.

For livestock farmers there is a restricted opportunity to take over another farmer's IACS return. The application form is IACS 18 and the guidance notes IACS 19.

In *R* v *MAFF, ex parte NFU and others* (Case C354/95) now in the European Court of Justice (unreported) a challenge has been mounted to the penalties levied by MAFF in the event of an honest mistake. The

Court held that the subsequent amendments to the scheme made in 1995 which reduced the penalties must be applied retroactively. The penalties applying to misstatements of forage area by more than 20% were upheld as not breaching the principles of proportionality, legal certainty and non-discrimination. The point at issue was the loss of all aid in the event of an honest error of 20% in the area of set-aside. In 1995 the penalties under the arable scheme were in fact reduced so that the area aid for arable crops was based on the set-aside area actually found.

Timing

It may be helpful to set out in tabular form some notes on timing. This is included in Appendix 7.

Social and Environmental Matters

Social and environmental aspects of the rural community are attracting increasing attention both nationally and on a European basis. Many of the conservation aspects previously dealt with on a national basis now fall within the overall European context.

The two principal European Regulations are:

Council Regulation 950/97 (OJ 1997 L142/1) on improving the efficiency of agricultural structures.

Council Regulation 2078/92 (OJ 1992 L215/95) on agricultural methods compatible with the requirements of the protection of the environment and the maintenance of the countryside ("the agri-environment Regulation") supplemented by Commission Regulation 746/96 (OJ 1996 L102/19) amended by Regulation 435/97 (OJ 1997 L67/2).

In addition there are various specific Directives such as Council Directive 91/676/EEC (OJ 1991 L375/1) concerning the protection of waters against pollution caused by nitrates from agricultural sources.

Environmental schemes need to be borne in mind on any transfer of occupation of farmland for example, on family rearrangements, sales of land, surrender or termination of tenancy and in the administration of deceased persons' estates. The detailed requirements vary from time to time but the Ministry is usually helpful. It is particularly important to comply with the requirements because, if they are breached, payments already made may be recovered. In most cases the occupier will have given undertakings for a certain period – clearly, on any change of occupation, these undertakings must be borne in mind and, usually, replacement undertakings if possible obtained.

Examples of schemes which may be relevant are:

Hill livestock compensatory allowances

These are regulated under the Hill Livestock (Compensatory Allowances) Regulations 1996 SI No 1500 amended by Hill Livestock (Compensatory Allowances) (Amendment) Regulations 1997, SI 1997 No 33.

An undertaking will have been given that the applicant will for five years continue to use eligible land for agricultural purposes. Retention periods apply.

On ceasing farming the applicant must liaise with MAFF to prevent recovery of HLCAs.

Moorland scheme

Regulated under SI 1995 No 904 Moorland (Livestock Extensification) Regulations amended by SI 1996 No 2393 Moorland (Livestock Extensification) (Amendment) Regulations 1996 and SI 1996 No 3110.

An undertaking will have been given that the applicant will for five years:

- limit the density of livestock;
- use adequate forage area;
- comply with certain management requirements.

On a change of occupation the applicant must notify MAFF within three months and secure a replacement undertaking from the new occupier, save where the applicant's occupation is terminated by the landlord terminating his tenancy (on death or otherwise) or by compulsory purchase.

Nitrate sensitive areas

Regulated under SI 1994 No 1729 Nitrate Sensitive Areas Regulations 1994 amended by SI 1995 No 1708, SI 1995 No 2095, SI 1996 No 3105 and SI 1997 No 990.

An undertaking will have been given to comply with management requirements for five years.

On a change of occupation the applicant must notify MAFF within three months and secure a new undertaking from the replacement occupier, save where the applicant's occupation is terminated by the termination of his tenancy by the landlord (on death or otherwise) or by compulsory purchase.

The rules are tightened and penalties imposed in the event of breach of an undertaking by the Nitrate Sensitive Areas (Amendment) Regulations 1996, SI 1996 No 3105.

Habitat scheme

Regulated under SI 1994 No 1291 Habitat (Water Fringe) Regulations 1994 amended by SI 1996 No 1480 and SI 1996 No 3106.

SI 1994 No 1292 Habitat (Former Set-Aside Land) Regulations 1994 amended by SI 1996 No 1478 and SI 1996 No 3107.

SI 1994 No 1293 Habitat (Salt Marsh) Regulations 1994 as amended by SI 1995 No 2871 and SI 1996 No 1479 and SI 1996 No 3108.

An undertaking will have been given to comply with management regulations for 20 years. On a change of occupation the applicant must notify MAFF within three months and secure a new undertaking from the replacement occupier, save where the applicant's occupation is terminated by the termination of his tenancy by the landlord (on death or otherwise) or by compulsory purchase.

Environmentally sensitive areas

Section 18 of the Agriculture Act 1986 amended by the Agriculture Act 1986 (Amendment) Regulations 1994, SI 1994 No 249. There are individual Statutory Instruments governing each Environmentally Sensitive Area.

Any person wishing to do so, who is occupying land in an Environmentally Sensitive Area may enter into a management agreement with MAFF which will last for 10 years with an option to terminate after five.

There are the usual requirements to ensure that a new occupier takes over responsibility for the agreement and repayment and penalty provisions in the event of breach of an agreement. These are tightened up by the Environmentally Sensitive Areas (England) Designation Order (Amendment) Regulations 1996, SI No 3104.

Farm woodland premium scheme

The Farm Woodland Premium Scheme 1992, SI No 905 was amended and replaced from 1 April 1997 by the Farm Woodland Premium Scheme 1997, SI 1997 No 829.

The applicant will give a management undertaking (*inter alia*) to maintain good forestry practice for 20 or 30 years (depending on the cover). The grant will be recovered if the undertaking is broken unless the breach is due to circumstances beyond the applicant's control *e.g.* death or compulsory purchase.

Countryside stewardship scheme

Applicants will give undertakings for varying periods. Notice of a change of occupation should be given within three months. Unless there is a reason beyond the applicant's control, aid may be recovered and a penalty levied unless a new occupier joins the scheme. The Government intends to use this scheme extensively. It is covered by the Countryside Stewardship Regulations 1996, SI 1996 No 695 amended by SI 1996 No 1481 and SI 1996 No 3123 made under the Environment Act 1995, section 48.

Countryside access scheme and guaranteed set aside

The applicant gives an undertaking for five years. The applicant must notify MAFF of any change in occupation and will be obliged to repay the aid unless the new occupier gives a replacement undertaking or the occupier's occupation was terminated by circumstances beyond his control *e.g.* termination of tenancy or compulsory purchase.

Countryside Access Regulations 1994, SI 1994 No 2349 as amended by SI 1996 No 3111.

Organic aid scheme

Under the Organic Farming (Aid) Regulations 1994, SI 1994 No 1721 amended by SI 1996 No 3109.

An undertaking will be given for five to nine years depending on the length of the conversion period. On a transfer of occupation MAFF must be notified and a new undertaking secured to protect the parties.

Management agreements

There may be management agreements under the woodland grant scheme the Wildlife and Countryside Act 1981 and various other statutes.

Normally action is required on a transfer of occupation to prevent aid previously paid being recovered.

Nitrate vulnerable zones

The future may be foreshadowed by the rules for these zones arising from the nitrate Directive. In certain designated areas there will be restrictions on user on an uncompensated basis. The action programmes are to be implemented by 19 December 1999. The United Kingdom has issued the Protection of Water against Agricultural Nitrate Pollution (England and Wales) Regulations 1996, SI 1996 No 888 to enable the preparatory work to proceed. A 25% grant is available for slurry disposal facilities under the Farm Waste Grant (Nitrate Vulnerable Zones) (England and Wales) Scheme 1996, SI 1996 No 908. A judicial review of one of the designations is in progress.

Hedgerows

Detailed regulations on hedgerows under section 97 Environment Act 1995 are now in force namely the Hedgerows Regulations 1997, SI 1997 No 1160. If any hedgerow is to be removed the local planning authority must first be informed. If the authority serves a "Hedgerow Retention Notice" the hedgerow cannot be removed, unless a successful appeal is made.

Many enclosure awards included provisions for the establishment and maintenance of hedgerows. Whether or not these provisions are still enforceable and by whom was considered in the County Court case of *Seymour* v *Flamborough Parish Council* (unreported). Unfortunately the Council was unable to finance the case and accordingly they were not represented. The judge sought nonetheless to consider both sides of the argument and decided that the obligation was enforceable still.

Animal Health - BSE

For some years the United Kingdom had regarded itself as one of the leaders in Europe in the field of animal health. Accordingly the BSE crisis and the ban on export of British beef has been a shocking experience. Domestic legislation stems now from the Animal Health Act 1981. One of the few positive aspects of the BSE crisis is that it has resulted in a heightening of standards Europe wide. It is not intended to provide a detailed exposition of animal health legislation. It may be helpful however to look at the BSE legislation and at some of the proposals for the future.

BSE

In March 1996 the export ban on British beef was imposed by the European Commission and BSE leapt to prominence.

The ban

This was imposed by Commission Decision 96/239/EC of 27 March 1996 (OJ 1996 L78/7). The ban was partially lifted in respect of gelatine and tallow by Commission Decision 96/362/EC of 11 June 1996 (OJ 1996 L139/17).

The legality of the ban is being fought by both the UK Government and the NFU. The Court of Justice rejected the Government's preliminary application in Case C 180/96 *United Kingdom* v *Commission* [1996] 3 CMLR 1. The Court of First Instance rejected the NFU'S application in Case T 76/96 *NFU* v *Commission* (Proceedings of the Court of Justice and the Court of First Instance 20/96 p55).

It will be some time before the issue is finally resolved and the outcome may be of little help to most farmers. The NFU has asked members to return a questionnaire if they have suffered loss. Should the ban be overturned they might be entitled to damages.

The plan

In order to make any progress towards the lifting of the ban the United Kingdom had to secure the Commission's agreement to its plans for the control and eradication of BSE. This was ultimately obtained by Commission Decision 96/385/EC of 24 June 1996 (OJ 1996 L151/39).

The principal elements of the plan are:

- selective slaughter of animals;
- control of movement and traceability of animals;
- control of the feed industry;
- veterinary studies of each affected herd.

Commission approval must be obtained of any change to the plan. No date has been fixed for the lifting of the ban. The United Kingdom has finally decided to continue with the plan.

UK restrictions

Under the Bovine Spongiform Encephalopathy (No 2) Order 1996, SI 1996 No 3183:

- infected animals must be notified and slaughtered;
- feed containing mammalian meat or bone meal must not be supplied or fed to animals.

Under the Fresh Meat (Beef Controls) Regulations (No 2) 1996, SI 1996 No 2097 amended by SI 1996 No 2522 Fresh Meat (Beef Controls) (No 2) (Amendment) Regulations 1996 meat from bovine animals having more than two permanent incisors erupted must not be sold for human consumption unless it can be proved that the animal is no more than 30 months old. There is an exception for beef comprised in the Beef Assurance Scheme under which animals can be slaughtered up to 42 months old.

The Bovine Animals (Records Identification and Movement) Order 1995, SI 1995 No 12 gave effect to Council Directive 92/102/EEC of 27 November 1992 (OJ 1992 L355/32) on the identification and registration of animals. This was amended and tightened up following the BSE crisis by the Cattle Passports Order 1996, SI 1996 No 1686. Cattle and calves can now be neither moved nor sold without an accompanying passport. In the case of cattle an application must be made within 28 days of ear tagging.

Selective slaughter scheme
For details see below.

Compensation provisions

Infected animals
Compensation is payable for infected animals under the Bovine Spongiform Encephalopathy Compensation Order 1996, SI 1996 No 3184.

30 month slaughter scheme
The Government has instituted a scheme for the slaughter of healthy stock in excess of 30 months old. The scheme is administered by the Intervention Board. The scheme is an EU scheme deriving authority from Commission Regulation 716/96 (OJ 1996 L99/14) amended by Regulations 774/96 (OJ 1996 L104/21), 835/96 (OJ 1996 L112/17), 1512/96 (OJ 1996 L189/3), 1846/96 (OJ 1996 L245/9), 1974/96 (OJ 1996 L262/2), 2149/96 (OJ 1996 L288/14), 2423/96 (OJ 1996 L329/43) and 1365/97 (OJ 1997 L188/6).

Calf processing aid scheme
The Government has also instituted a scheme for the slaughter and payment of compensation for bull calves withdrawn from production before attaining the age of 20 days. Again this is an EU scheme deriving authority from the following:

Article 4i Council Regulation 805/68 (OJ 1968 L148/24) amended by Regulations 2066/92 (OJ 1992 L215/49) and 1357/96 (OJ 1996 L175/9).

Commission Regulation 3886/92 (OJ 1992 L391/20) as amended.

Commission Decision 96/503/EC of 26 July 1996 (OJ 1996 L204/19).

The Scheme is administered by the Intervention Board.

Top up payments
There have been various top up payments for cattle sold after the crises under the Beef (Marketing Payment) Regulations under Council Regulation 1357/96 (above).

Selective slaughter scheme
It is intended to locate all animals "associated" by "birth cohort" with a confirmed BSE animal. When a case of BSE occurred after September 1990 all animals in the same birth cohort will be traced and slaughtered. The scheme is administered by the Intervention Board who have published a guide to the scheme although MAFF has some responsibilities. The EU authority for the scheme is Commission

Regulation 1484/96 (OJ 1996 L188/25). The UK authority is the Bovine Spongiform Encephalopathy Order 1996, SI 1996 No 3184.

Offences are dealt with in the UK regulation The Selective Cull (Enforcement of Community Compensation Conditions) Regulations 1996, SI 1996 No 3186.

Payments under beef special premium and suckler cow premium schemes

Payments to producers under these schemes have been topped up. The EU authority is Regulation 1357/96 (above).

Beef assurance scheme

This scheme is set up under the Fresh Meat (Beef Controls) (No 2) Regulations 1996, SI 1996 No 2097 amended by the Fresh Meat (Beef Controls) (No 2) (Amendment) Regulations 1996, SI 1996 No 2522. It applies to separate beef herds satisfying the following requirements:

1. Separate management on the ground.
2. No animals kept reared or used for milk production shall have been present on the same holding within seven years prior to the application.
3. There are no confirmed cases of BSE:
   - in the herd;
   - in animals originating from the herd;
   - in any herd to which animals in the applicant's herd have ever belonged.
4. The herd has existed for four years.
5. No animal has within seven years been fed feed containing meat and bone meal.
6. No animal has within four years been fed compound feed subject to some exceptions.

There are restrictions on the animals which can be added to the herd and management and notification requirements.

Presumably this certification is likely to be very valuable. Farmers who think they may qualify must be careful not to add to the holding areas which might trigger a breach of the second requirement. This should be considered before land is rented or purchased certainly until it is clear exactly how it will be interpreted. Furthermore great care must be taken in adding animals to the herd to protect BSE-free status. Clearly stringent checks and warranties will be required. There is a booklet BAS 1 published by MAFF.

The future

Council Directive 97/12/EC of 17 March 1979 (OJ 1997 L109/1) replaces Directive 64/432/EEC relating to health problems affecting intra Community trade in bovine animals and swine with effect from 1 July 1998. It contains provisions relating to documentation, health and transport and provides a power for Member States to introduce a surveillance system. It goes on to provide that there must be a computer database operated in all Member States by 31 December 1999.

Council Regulation 820/97 (OJ 1997 L117/1) contains further rules as to identification and registration of bovine animals including documentation regulations coming into effect on 11 July 1997. The regulations affect animals born after 11 January 1998. Furthermore it provides for the introduction of a compulsory beef labelling system with effect from 1 January 2000. The supplemental Commission Regulation is 1141/97 (OJ 1997 L165).

No doubt traceability and record keeping will be greatly improved. Hopefully the benefits can be obtained at reasonable expense.

Commission Decision 97/534 of 30 July 1997 (OJ 1997 L216/95) makes provision for destruction of the skull including the brain and eyes, tonsils and spinal cord of bovine animals aged over 12 months and ovine and caprine animals aged over 12 months or having a permanent incisor tooth erupted and also the spleen of ovine and caprine animals. This applies throughout the Community pending further scientific evidence.

Transport requirements are tightened up by the Welfare of Animals (Transport) Order 1997, SI No 1480 in the light of updated EU legislation.

PART 5

Taxation

It is not intended here to provide a detailed discussion of taxation. However, there are some points which need to be borne in mind in structuring arrangements for farmers and country landowners. Some of them are collected here. If a particular point is of relevance, it should be checked with the appropriate specialised text book as it is possible only to give a broad outline here.

The topics discussed are:

1. Leasing quota
2. Short rotation coppice and habitat scheme land
3. Inheritance tax
4. Capital gains tax
5. Valuation of agricultural tenancies
6. Transactions with developers
7. Value added tax.
8. Income tax
9. Compensation for disturbance

Leasing quota

Leasing out quota may mean that the Revenue regards the quota not as a business asset but as an investment. This could affect seriously inheritance tax and capital gains tax reliefs. The fiscal effects of leasing should therefore be considered.

Short rotation coppice and habitat schemes

There is a specific provision that this shall be treated for fiscal purposes as agriculture (s 154 Finance Act 1995). Section 94 of the Finance Act 1997 provides similarly for land subject to the habitat schemes.

CHAPTER 18

Inheritance Tax

Agricultural relief

Now that 100% relief is available for inheritance tax purposes in appropriate cases it is crucial to make sure that this relief is available and, if not, to see what steps can be taken to obtain it.

It is necessary to remember the rules both for agricultural relief and for business relief. This is particularly important where, for example, there is land with planning potential. The planning potential would not attract agricultural relief but would attract business relief. To obtain 100% relief on that land it would have to be an asset of the business qualifying for business relief.

The specific rules for agricultural relief are contained in sections 115–124 (B) Inheritance Tax Act 1984 as amended.

The assets attracting 100% relief are:

- Shares in a private company. It is necessary to check whether there are any non-business assets owned by the company. If there is a lot of cash pending reinvestment it may nonetheless be possible to obtain relief on this. However the intention to reinvest will have to be proved. *Brown's Executors* v *IRC* (1996) STC (STC) 277.
- An interest in a business. Again it is necessary to check whether there are any non-business assets for example a large stock of cash.
- Land held with vacant possession or the right to obtain it within twelve months. The period is now extended by concession to two years and other situations where property is valued broadly at vacant possession value. *Simon's Tax Intelligence* of 16 February 1995, p7. It is necessary to ensure that one falls within the concession.
- Land which was let in 1981 and subject to the transitional provisions and would have obtained relief at that time.
- Land let after 1 September 1995 (s 116 Inheritance Tax Act 1984 as amended by s 155 FA1995).

Tenancies

If there is a tenancy which prevents 100% relief applying then it is worth considering whether something should be done about it, although some people prefer to preserve the status quo on the basis that the rules are quite likely to change again. In order to remove the tenancy it is necessary for the freehold and the tenancy to end up in the same hands. This can be done either by the tenant acquiring the freehold or by the tenant surrendering the tenancy. In the latter case it will apparently not be regarded as a PET attracting 100% relief because as the asset disappears it has not been retained by the acquirer for the requisite seven year period. Also, the 1982 base value of the tenancy may be "lost".

Non-agricultural use

The Revenue is taking the point that properties have to be appropriate to the land in question. A mansion house therefore with five acres is unlikely to attract agricultural relief whereas a cottage with 50 acres probably would. Care must be taken therefore if the farm house is to be split off from the holding.

Starke & Another v IRC (1995) EGCS 91

In this case a farmhouse with 2.5 acres and buildings (used with a farm of 150-200 acres) did not attract relief.

Similarly, agricultural relief will not be available if diversification into small business units has taken place. Likewise, cottages which are let off on short-hold will not attract relief. The position is clarified by concession confirming that relief applies to cottages occupied by retired farm employees and their spouses so long as the occupation is statutorily protected (*Simon's Tax Intelligence* of 16 February 1995, p256). In *GW Harrold Exors v CIR* (1996) STC (SCD) 195 a gift of farmland included a farmhouse not in use at the time of the gift. Relief was denied because the property was not "occupied" with the land.

Creation of tenancies

The Capital Taxes Office is still interested in the formation of tenancies. If they were in existence in 1974 then no problem arises. If they were created after that date the Capital Taxes Office will wish to make sure that they were granted for full consideration as otherwise they may argue that a transfer of value took place which was never returned. The tax and interest if this happens can be very significant.

Partnership and shareholders' agreements

Some partnership agreements and shareholders' agreements require a deceased person's personal representatives to sell out. This is likely to constitute a "buy and sell" agreement which will result in the loss of relief. Such agreements should be checked and, if necessary, options substituted.

Retention of assets

If lifetime gifts are made it is essential to remember that the transferee must retain the assets (or comply with the restrictive replacement rules) for seven years after the gift. This includes trustees and therefore removal of property from trusts within this period and transfer to beneficiaries can be a problem, even if it occurs simply on the beneficiary satisfying a contingency such as attaining a specified age.

Reservation of benefit

The rules regarding reservation of benefit must also be borne in mind. For example, if land is given away and the donor remains involved in the business, a full rental must be paid. This must continue until the donor retires from the business or dies. An interesting case on carving out a leasehold interest for the donor is *Ingram* v *IRC* (1995) STC 564. It is believed that the Revenue is to appeal.

Ownership and occupation requirements

It is important to remember the need for ownership for seven years or occupation for two years in order to obtain relief. The tenant who buys in the freehold may interestingly obtain immediate relief on the freehold because of the occupation requirement.

Security

It is desirable to try and secure agricultural borrowings on non-relieved assets to maximise relief.

CHAPTER 19

Capital Gains Tax

Although at first sight tax rates for income tax and capital gains tax are now the same there are various reliefs for capital gains which are extremely important. It is therefore essential to consider whether matters are organised in the best way to achieve tax savings in future.

Rollover relief

Rollover relief is available when an asset used in the business is sold and replaced. The landowner concerned has to be trading on the land or a shareholder with at least 5% of the shares in a company farming the land. Thus for example, non-trading trusts will not be able to claim. If rollover is important the land ownership must be appropriately structured. The time limits (one year before and three years after) must also be watched carefully. *Anderton* v *Lamb* (1981) STC 43 highlights a possible problem. There rollover relief was denied on houses occupied by partners in a farming business as they were considered not to be business assets. It is worth considering whether an appropriate clause in the partnership agreement is desirable or private residence relief can be claimed.

In *Watton* v *Tippett* reported in *Simon's Weekly Tax Intelligence*, 14 December 1995, p1996 rollover relief was considered. There the tax payer bought some property and traded from it. Subsequently, he sold part of the property and sought to roll over the capital gain into the original purchase. It was held in the Chancery Division that rollover was not available because the rollover was into the same asset and not "other assets". It would seem therefore that if a subsequent sale is intended the purchase should, if possible, be by separate contracts. Even so it would presumably be open to the Revenue to argue that the gain on a sale within 12 months (required for rollover purposes) was not a capital transaction but an income transaction.

In transactions affecting dairy farms a tenancy is often put in place. If a purchaser buys a holding subject to such a tenancy he will not be able to claim rollover relief because the new asset is not "taken into use" in the business: *Campbell Connelly & Co Ltd* v *Barnett* (1994) STC 50 – a case in a retail context demonstrating the problem. This must not be overlooked.

Retirement relief

Retirement relief is available when an individual disposes of an asset used in the business as part of his disposal of the business or indeed when an individual disposes of the business itself. The requirements are restrictive and have to be carefully complied with but the prize is large, a tax free gain of £250,000 together with relief on half the excess of the gain up to £1,000,000.

Payment of rent will interfere with the relief and it will not be available on the disposal of an asset used in the business rather than part of the business itself. Retirement relief was the subject of *Plumbly and others v Spencer* (1996) STC (SCD) 295. There land was owned by a director and let to a company. The land was sold and the company ceased trading. No disposal of shares was made. An ingenious argument that what is now Section 163(2) TCGA 1992 afforded relief failed. There has been a number of cases on this.

McGregor v Adcock (1977) 3 All ER 65
4.8 acres were sold out of a holding of 35 acres. It was held to be the disposal of an asset of the business not a part of the business and therefore no retirement relief was available.

Atkinson v Dancer, Mannion v Johnston (1988) STC 758
Atkinson farmed on 22 acres of freehold and 67 acres of leasehold land. He sold nine acres of the freehold. Johnston farmed 78 acres. He sold 17 acres and eight months later 18 acres. In both cases relief was denied.

Pepper v Daffurn (1993) STC 466
Daffurn had 113 acres. He sold 83. There was a covered yard on what was left. He ran down his herd over two years and then sold the yard. Thereafter he grazed cattle instead of rearing. Relief on the yard was denied.

Jarmin v Rawlings (1994) STC 1005
This case went the other way. There the tax payer was a dairy farmer who owned 64 acres of land, milking parlour, yard, hay barn, sheds and 34 cattle. In October 1988 he sold the milking parlour and yard at auction. Between then and completion in January 1987 14 cows were sold. The balance was transferred to his sister's farm and sold gradually. He took no benefit from their milk after January 1989. Thereafter, the tax payer reared and finished store cattle. It was held by Knox J that the Special Commissioners could have regarded the sale as a sale of a dairy farming

business and the sale of the parlour and yards as a sale of part of a business. Retirement relief was therefore available.

Wase v Bourke (1996) STC 18 ChD
Retirement relief was denied. The tax payer sold his dairy herd in March 1988 and then his quota in February 1989. The judge held the sale of the quota was a sale of an asset in the business not a disposal of part of the business and it did not satisfy the "simultaneous disposal" test. The taxpaper did not satisfy the age requirement in March 1988.

Care must be taken both to structure the business appropriately and to review the disposal process.

Indexation relief

Indexation from 1982 is very significant and given agricultural values at that time is usually crucially important on a disposal. Now indexation losses cannot in general be carried forward and it is therefore essential to use them so far as possible.

Where there is a part disposal it is often better to calculate the gain on the $\frac{A}{A + B}$ basis where A is the sale price of the property sold and B the value of the property retained. By doing this a gain on the sale of say a cottage can often be reduced or eliminated.

Where the land is standing at a considerable loss and there are cottages or development land an "in house" disposal of the whole can be considered so that the loss can be fully used.

Trading in land?

Care must be taken if a tenant buys the freehold and then sells on with vacant possession. On the face of it this is a trading transaction and it would be better to structure it so that there is clearly a capital disposal of the tenancy rather than a trading transaction.

Private residence relief

This may be relevant in an agricultural context. If there is planning permission on the garden it may be necessary to sell the plot before the house and not vice versa.

Reinvestment relief

The recent lifting of restrictions on reinvestment relief may well increase the scope to defer capital gains tax liability. Where a capital gain arises the opportunity to use this should always be explored. However, the antiavoidance provisions are tricky and need to be watched.

Surrender and regrant

The implications of surrender and regrant of tenancies from a Capital Gains Tax point of view should be considered. If the surrender is a disposal of the old tenancy will this lead to a tax charge? The new tenancy is likely to be a new asset with possibly a base value of nil. In *Bayley* v *Rogers* (1980) STC 544 in the context of the Landlord and Tenant Act 1954 a new statutory tenancy was held not to be a continuation of the old tenancy for Capital Gains Tax purposes.

CHAPTER 20

Valuation of Agricultural Tenancies

There have been three significant cases on the valuation of tenancies for tax purposes.

Baird's Executors v IRC
(CTT News and Reports September 1990 p122 Scottish Lands Tribunal decision).

Since 1959 George Alexander Baird and his son George Donald Baird had been jointly entitled to a tenancy of the farm of Mains of Dun Montrose. On 24 September 1977 the son was killed in a car accident. On 9 December 1977 the father renounced the tenancy by a letter to the landlord of the farm requesting that it be transferred into the names of his daughter-in-law and grandson. The landlord agreed and the land was subsequently farmed by the daughter-in-law and grandson in partnership with the father. The Inland Revenue contended that the renunciation was a chargeable transfer for the purposes of capital transfer tax as it then was and that the value transfered was £138,000. The Executors disputed the claim on the grounds that:

1. The tenancy had no value because it could not be transferred without consent; and
2. The transferor's interest was only in one half of the tenancy.

The Lands Tribunal held that clearly a tenancy had a value. Since the tax payer had adduced no evidence of its value they had to accept the District Valuer's figure. They agreed, however, that only half of the tenancy had to be valued.

Executors of John Hedley Walton v CIR 1996 STC 68 CA
John Hedley Walton (the deceased) died on 6 August 1984. His sons, Frederick and John, were his executors. At the date of his death the deceased, Frederick and John owned the freehold in Keepwick Farm Northumberland as tenants in common in equal shares. The farm was let to a partnership between the deceased and John under a written agreement. John was aged 36 with an estimated life expectancy of 37 years. The benefit of the tenancy was to pass to the continuing partner so far as practicable.

In August 1984 the yearly rent reserved was £6,000 and it was liable to increase by arbitration on 13 May 1986.

In August 1984 the estimated arbitration rental value was £8,250 and the tender rental value was £12,000. The vacant possession value of the farm was £400,000 but the value of the freehold subject to the tenancy was £150,000.

The transcript states that the vacant possession premium was £200,000 (although this does not seem to stack up with the other valuations). The value of tenantright and tenants improvements less dilapidations was £40,000 and these were assets of the partnership.

The tribunal decided that it was necessary to look at the situation in each individual case. In this particular case they were satisfied that no money would be forthcoming from the landlord and therefore on the notional sale valuing the tenancy they felt that the realisation of any sum by reference to vacant possession would be so far from any market expectation as to be inappropriate. As the purchaser would take subject to the non-assignability both of the tenancy and his partnership share all he could do would be to retire which would not result in any realisation of market value of the tenancy. The only value therefore of the tenancy as an asset of the partnership depended upon the extent to which its terms would enhance the profits of the partnership. In the end the tribunal decided that the tenancy was worth £12,645 plus a sum to be agreed in respect of improvements and tenantright. They saw no need to make a deduction for it being a partnership asset. They did not see John as a likely purchaser and therefore valued the deceased's share in the partnership so far as related to the tenancy at £6,300. The Revenue's appeal was dismissed by the Court of Appeal.

Robin Gray v CIR (The Lady Fox Case) (1994) 38 EG 156
This is a Court of Appeal decision on appeal from the Lands Tribunal and therefore more authoritative than *Baird* and *Walton*.

Lady Fox died on 27 March 1981. She owned the freehold of the 3,000 acre Croxton Park Estate in Cambridgeshire which was let to a farming partnership in which she had a 92.5% interest. The other partners were Major Fraser a retired army officer aged 61 who had a 2.5% interest in the profits and Edward Crees a partner of Strutt & Parker aged 57, who also farmed on his own account and had a 5% share of the profits.

The Revenue argued that the freehold and the partnership should be valued together for the purpose of inheritance tax. The District Valuer estimated that the surrender value of the tenancy was £1.5 million being about 45% of the additional value created by adding it to the freehold.

The freehold was worth £6.125 million with vacant possession and £2.751 million tenanted. The District Valuer valued the 7.5% interest in the tenancy at £100,000. Accordingly the hypothetical purchaser who bought the freehold and partnership share could reasonably reckon on obtaining vacant possession by laying out that sum for the tenancy. To allow for difficulties, however, the District Valuer deducted another £460,000 or 7.5% of the vacant possession value. On that basis he concluded that as the estate with vacant possession was worth £6.125 million the hypothetical purchaser would have paid £560,000 less for the tenanted freehold and Lady Fox's interest in the partnership so far as it was attributable to the tenancy. This produced a figure of £5.565 million of which the District Valuer thought that £4,280,768 should be apportioned to the freehold interest and the balance of £1,284,232 to the tenancy. The Court held that the Revenue's approach was right. It was necessary to value both assets together as this was likely to produce the best deal on the hypothetical sale. The Court was not convinced that the valuation itself was right since the Lands Tribunal had expressed some doubt as to whether the deduction was big enough. There was, however, no additional evidence adduced on behalf of the taxpayer as to this and therefore the Court had no option but to uphold the Revenue's valuation.

It seems that the valuation of tenancies for tax purposes now may depend very much on the circumstances and the attitude of the landlord in each case. The Revenue will be reviewing its practice and great care is needed. The Revenue has issued guidance (*Simon's Weekly Tax Intelligence*, 22 August 1996, p1369). This underlines the possible discrepancy betwen 1982 valuations and disposal values.

Farm business tenancies

The valuation of farm business tenancies is different. A tenancy at a full rent with no security of tenure will have no value. Even a term tenancy may be treated as a wasting asset for capital gains tax purposes. This means rollover will be temporary. We must await experience in practice.

CHAPTER 21

Transactions with Developers

As the market for potential development land seems to be recovering, developers are encouraging landowners once again to enter into joint ventures and option agreements. Some points of difficulty may be worth mentioning.

Joint Ventures

These usually involve a pooling of resources and a division of profits when the land is finally developed and sold.

It is essential to avoid an immediate disposal which would attract tax taking place by mistake. The terms should be checked to ensure that this is not happening.

The Revenue may argue that the land has been appropriated to trading stock. While the owner can elect to avoid any tax at this stage the ultimate profit would be income taxable not a capital gain. This means that the valuable reliefs *e.g.* rollover, retirement relief and indexation are not available.

Options

A developer often seeks an option to acquire land exercisable on obtaining planning permission. If the option is given for value that will be a disposal chargeable to capital gains tax. When the option is exercised there is a disposal of the land. Thus the tax regime at that time will apply and the tax rates could then be higher. It is best to give the donor the opportunity to defeat or postpone the exercise if the tax would exceed a certain proportion of the sale proceeds.

Conditional contracts

Sometimes the arrangement proposed takes the form of a conditional contract. It is important to check whether the condition is a condition precedent or a condition subsequent. The distinction is not very clear but essentially there should be no binding sale contract until the condition is satisfied. If this can be arranged the disposal will be at the time the condition is satisfied rather than at the time the contract is signed.

Deferred consideration

There is often provision for deferred consideration. There is the practical problem of ensuring that it is secured by some form of mortgage. Also the Revenue will regard the disposal as made at the contract date and collect tax accordingly. It is therefore essential to ensure that enough cash is received in time to pay the tax (s 48 Taxation of Chargeable Gains Act 1992).

If the consideration is unquantified the Revenue may value the right to receive it and add that to the consideration. When the consideration is finally received there will be a further disposal creating a profit or loss. Rollover and retirement relief will not be available on the subsequent disposal. See *Marron* v *Ingles* (1980) STC 500.

CHAPTER 22

Value Added Tax

Election to tax

Some landlords are advised to elect to tax their estates to enable them to recover VAT on expenditure on buildings and professional fees. Care should be taken because of the need to charge VAT on rent and on disposals out of the estate and the possible disadvantageous effect on future transactions. Election on part of an estate is now possible and this may be very useful in practice.

De minimis rule

Where a person is registered as a trader he can reclaim VAT paid on certain expenditure not otherwise reclaimable provided it falls within the *de minimis* rules. Section 106 VAT regulations 1995, SI 1995 No 2518. The amount is currently £625 per month on average. It must also be less than 50% of all input tax. Relevant expenditure should if possible be phased to take advantage of this.

Farmhouses

Guidelines have been published on the recoverability of VAT on repairs, maintenance and renovation of farmhouses (*Simon's Weekly Tax Intelligence*, 5 September 1996, p1441).

CHAPTER 23

Income Tax

The question of whether growing Christmas trees constitutes woodland management or a trade was considered in *Jaggers* v *Ellis* (1996) STC (SCD) 440. The Special Commissioners decided that on the facts of that case the growing of Christmas trees was a trade taxable under Schedule D Case 1 and not woodlands outside the charge to income tax. Each case will turn on its facts.

CHAPTER 24

Compensation

Compensation for disturbance payable under section 60 of the Agriculture Holdings Act 1986 is tax free: *Davis* v *Powell* [1977] 1 All ER 471.

This was reinstated in *Davis* v *Henderson* (1995) Sp C 308 and *Pritchard* v *Purves* (1995) Sp C 316. Revenue guidance has been published reprinted at *Simon's Tax Intelligence*, 2 May 1996, p793. Essentially the notice to quit procedure must be followed; a surrender agreement labelling the payment "compensation for disturbance" will not suffice.

Appendix I

Milk Quotas

Article 7 Council Regulation 3950/92 (OJ 1992 L405/1)

1.   Reference quantities available on a holding shall be transferred with the holding in the case of sale, lease or transfer by inheritance to the producers taking it over in accordance with detailed rules to be determined by the Member States taking account of the areas used for dairy production or other objective criteria and, where applicable, of any agreement between the parties. Any part of the reference quantity which is not transferred with the holding shall be added to the national reserve.

The same provisions shall apply to other cases of transfer involving comparable legal effects for producers.

However:

(a)   until 30 June 1994, the reference quantity referred to in Article 4(3) (Slom quota) shall be added to the national reserve in the case of sale or leasing of the holding;

(b)   where land is transferred to public authorities and/or for use in the public interest, or where the transfer is carried out for non-agricultural purposes, Member States shall provide that the measures necessary to protect the legitimate interests of the parties are implemented, and in particular that the departing producer is in a position to continue milk production, if such is his intention.

2.   Where there is no agreement between the parties, in the case of rural leases due to expire without any possibility of renewal on similar terms, or in situations involving comparable legal effects, the reference quantities available on the holdings in question shall be transferred in whole or in part to the producers taking them over, in accordance with provisions adopted or to be adopted by the Member States, taking account of the legitimate interests of the parties.

Appendix 2

Beef Special Premium Scheme

Article 4b of Regulation 805/68 (OJ 1968 L148/24)†

1.   A producer holding male bovine animals on his holding may qualify, on application, for a special premium. It shall be granted in the form of an annual premium per calendar year per holding within the limits of regional ceilings for not more than 90 animals for each of the age brackets referred to in paragraph 2.

2.   The premium shall be granted no more than:

(a)   once in the life of each uncastrated male bovine animal from 10 to 21 months old; or

(b)   twice in the life of each castrated male bovine animal:
- the first time at the age of 10 months,
- the second time after it has reached the age of 22 months.

To qualify for the premium, any animal covered by an application must be held for fattening for a period to be determined.

3.   When in a given region the total number of animals for which an application has been made and which satisfy the conditions for granting the special premium exceeds the regional ceiling, the number of eligible animals per producer for the year in question shall be reduced proportionally.

When calculating the total number account shall be taken only of animals in the 10 to 21 month age bracket for which an application has been made.

Within the meaning of this Article, the following definitions shall apply:

(a)   "region"; a Member State or region within a Member State at the choice of the Member State concerned;

(b)   "regional ceiling"; the number of animals entitled to benefit, in a region and per calendar year, from the special premium; the total number of animals included in the regional ceilings of each of the Member States is limited to:

Belgium	293,211
Denmark	324,652
Germany	2,966,619
Greece	140,130
Spain including the Canary Islands	551,552
France	1,908,922

† As substituted by Reg 2066/92 (OJ 1992 L215/49) and amended by Reg 1884/94 (OJ 1994 L197/27) and Reg 2222/96 (OJ 1996 L296/50).

Ireland	1,286,521
Italy	824,885
Luxembourg	19,300
Netherlands	264,000
Portugal	154,897
United Kingdom	1,419,811

However, for 1997 and 1998, the following regional ceilings shall apply:

Belgium	235,149
Denmark	277,110
Germany (including the specific regional ceiling for the special premium referred to in Article 4k(1)(a), applicable to the new Länder)	1,782,700
Greece	140,130
Spain	603,674
France	1,754,732
Ireland	1,002,458
Italy	598,746
Luxembourg	18,962
Netherlands	157,932
Austria	423,400
Portugal	154,897
Finland	241,553
Sweden	226,328
United Kingdom	1,419,811

4.   Where the Member States have the necessary information, they may allocate to all producers individual ceilings within the limits of the Member States' regional ceilings and on the basis of objective criteria. In such cases:

(a)   each producer's right to premium shall be limited to his individual ceiling;

(b)   the proportional reduction shall not apply;

(c)   the Member States shall lay down special management conditions on the basis of the principles laid down in Articles 4e and 4f.

5.   Member States may decide to grant the premium at the time of slaughter. In this case, for uncastrated male bovine animals the age criteria referred to in paragraph 2(a) shall be replaced by a minimum weight of 200 kilo-grammes.

The premium shall be paid or passed back to the producers.

The United Kingdom shall be authorized to apply in Northern Ireland a system for granting the special premium which differs from that applied in the remainder of its territory.

6.   The premium per eligible animal shall be:

ECU 108,7 per castrated male animal,

ECU 135 per uncastrated male animal.

Save in duly justified exceptional cases, payment must be made as soon as the inspections are carried out and not later than 30 June of the year following the calendar year in respect of which the premium is applied for.

7.   At the latest from the time of the first premium application, each male bovine animal must be covered by an administrative document until slaughter.

7a.   Notwithstanding paragraph 2(a), Member States may choose to grant the premium for a second time in the life of each uncastrated male bovine animal, for a transitional period comprising the calendar years 1997 and 1998, up to a maximum of 3% of the number of animals in their regional ceilings. In that case, the premium shall be granted only:

  – after the animal concerned has reached the age of 22 months, and
  – provided that it has ben reared in a traditional extensive production region in the Member State concerned.

The second premium shall be ECU 81 per eligible animal.

8.   Detailed rules for applying this Article shall be adopted by the Commission in accordance with the procedure laid down in Article 27.

Commission Regulation 3886/92 (OJ 1992 L391/20)†

Article 2 – Applications

1. In addition to the requirements introduced as part of the integrated system, each "livestock" aid application (hereinafter called "application") shall contain:

(a) a breakdown of the number of animals by age bracket;

(b) the reference to the administrative documents accompanying the animals which are the subject of the application.

2. Applications may be submitted in respect only of animals which on the date of commencement of the retention period are:

> not less than eight months and not more than 20 months old in the case of the single age bracket, or

> in the case of castrated male bovine animals, not less than eight months and not more than 20 months old in the case of the first age bracket, or at least 21 months only in the case of the second age bracket.

Article 3 – Administrative Documents

1. Member States shall adopt the measures necessary to ensure that each animal is accompanied, at the latest from the date on which the first premium application is made, by a national administrative document. Such document shall in particular enable steps to be taken to ensure that one premium only is granted per animal and per age bracket.

2. Member States may provide that the national administrative document shall take the form of:

> – a document accompanying each individual animal,

> – a comprehensive list, held by the producer, of all the information required for the administrative document, on condition that the animals concerned remain, from the date on which the first application is made, with the same producer until they are placed on the market for the purpose of being slaughtered,

> – a comprehensive list, held by the central authorities, of all the information required for the administrative document, on condition that the Member State availing itself of this possibility carries out on-the-spot checks on all the animals covered by an application, checks the movements of those animals and makes a distinctive mark (ear punching) on each animal checked which the producers shall be required to permit.

> Member States which decide to avail themselves of one of these possibilities shall notify the Commission thereof in due time and forward to it the relevant implementing provisions. For the purposes of this paragraph, Great Britain and Northern Ireland alone shall be considered to be regions of a Member State.

3. For each animal likely to qualify for a premium and which is the subject of intra-Community trade, the Member State from which the animal comes shall

† Amended by Reg 538/93 (OJ 1993 L57/19) and Reg 2311/96 (OJ 1996 L313).

issue, on request to be submitted prior to the transaction, an administrative trade document, a model of which is set out in Annex I.

On the basis of the administrative trade document, the Member State of arrival shall issue, on request, a national administrative document.

However, where the national administrative document of a Member State corresponds in all ways with the above mentioned model, it may be used directly as an administrative trade document provided that it bears a heading to that effect.

4.   Member States shall assist one another in ensuring that the authenticity of administrative trade documents submitted is effectively checked.

Article 4 – Retention period

The duration of the retention period shall be two months starting on the date following the date of lodging of the application.

However, Member States may provide that other starting dates may be set by the producer provided that they do not occur more than two months after the date of lodging of the application.

Article 5 – Regional ceiling

1.   Where the application of the proportional reduction gives a number of eligible animals which is less than a whole number, there shall be granted in respect of the decimal part a corresponding fraction of the unit amount of the premium. For this purpose account shall be taken of the first decimal place only.

2.   Member States shall inform the Commission

(a)   by 30 June 1993 at the latest:
    – of the regions specified
    – of the number of male bovine animals in each region constituting the regional ceiling

(b)   by 30 June at the latest of each calendar year, of the number of animals broken down by age bracket for which the special premium has not been granted in respect of the previous calendar year on account of the application of the regional ceiling.

Article 6 – Individual ceiling

Before deciding to allocate individual ceilings, Member States shall notify the Commission thereof and shall inform them of the criteria adopted in this connection.

Article 7 – Grant of premium

1.   For the grant of the premium, account shall be taken
    – only of animals which are accompanied by their national administrative document, and
    – which are duly identified in accordance with the relevant national and Community provisions.

2.   Animals which have not qualified for the premium either on account of the application of the proportional reduction referred to in Article 4b (3) of Regulation (EEC) No 805/68 or of the application of the density factor may no longer be the subject of an application for the same age bracket and shall be considered to have received the premium.

Appendix 3

Suckler Cow Premium Scheme

Commission Regulation 3888/92 (OJ 1992 L391/46)
Article 2
1. For the purposes of this Regulation:
(a) A parcel of land that both contains trees and is used for crop production covered by Article 1 of Regulation (EEC) No 3508/92 shall be considered agricultural land, provided that production can be carried out in a similar way as on parcels without trees in the same area
(b) Where a forage area is used in common, the competent authorities shall assign it between the individual farmers in proportion to their use of it.
(c) Each forage area must be available for raising livestock for a minimum period of seven months, starting on a date to be determined by the Member State, which must be between 1 January and 31 March.
2. The competent authority shall consider several holdings as a single holding if separation has been carried out after 30 June 1992 where, taking account of all the economic and legal aspects of the case in question, this has been done principally to evade individual limits on eligibility for premiums referred to in Articles 4a to 4k of Regulation (EEC) No 805/68.
The preceding subparagraph shall not apply where the interested parties are able to prove a substantial change in the physical or financial structure of the holdings which could, in itself, justify the transformation of the holding in its previous form.
3. For the purposes of the integrated system, if a forage area is situated in a Member State other than that in which the principal place of business of the producer using it is situated, that area shall be deemed at the request of the applicant to be part of the holding of that producer provided:
  – it is situated in the immediate vicinity of the holding, and
  – the relative majority of all the agricultural land used by that producer is situated in the Member State in which he/she has his/her principal place of business.

Regulation No. 805/68†

Article 4a

For the purposes of this section:

– "producer" shall mean an individual farmer, whether a natural or a legal person or group of natural or legal persons, irrespective of the legal status conferred by national law on such a group or its members, whose holding is located in Community territory and who is engaged in rearing bovine animals,

"holding" shall mean all the production units managed by the producer and located in the territory of a single Member State,

"suckler cow" shall mean:

(i)   a cow belonging to a meat breed or born of a cross with a meat breed, and belonging to a herd intended for rearing calves for meat production;

and

(ii)   an in-calf heifer, meeting the same criteria, which replaces a suckler cow.

Article 4d

1.   A producer keeping suckler cows on his holding may qualify, on application, for a premium for maintaining suckler cows (suckler cow premium).

2.   The producers' right to the premium shall be limited by the application of an individual ceiling. This ceiling shall be equal to the number of animals for which a premium was granted in respect of the reference year, reduced so that the national reserve referred to in Article 4f may be set up. Member States may select 1990, 1991 or 1992 as the reference year. The Member States shall inform the Commission by 31 January 1993 of the reference year selected.

3.   In the event of natural circumstances resulting in a non-payment or a reduced payment of the premium for the reference year, the number adopted may be that corresponding to the payments made during the nearest reference year.

In the event of non-payment or reduced payment of the premium for the reference year, following the applications of the relevant penalties, the number adopted shall be that recorded at the time of the inspection which gave rise to those penalties.

4.   The right to premium shall apply to producers to whom the premium was granted in respect of the reference year and who also requested the premium for the years up to and including 1992.

5.   The premium shall be granted to any producer not supplying milk or milk products from his farm for twelve months from the day on which the application is lodged and who keeps for at least six consecutive months from the day on which the application is lodged a number of suckler cows at least equal to the number for which the premium was requested.

† As substituted by Reg 2066/92 and amended by Reg 125/93 (OJ 1993 L18/1) and Reg 3611/93 (OJ 1993 L328/7).

The supply of milk or milk products directly from the holding to the consumer shall not, however, prevent grant of the premium.

6.   The premium shall also be granted to any producer supplying milk or milk products whose individual reference quantity as referred to in Article 5c of Regulation (EEC) No 804/68 does not exceed 120,000 kilograms provided that he keeps, for at least six consecutive months from the day on which the application is lodged, a number of suckler cows at least equal to the number for which the premium was requested.

Additional rights to the suckler cow premium shall be added to the national reserves. The total number of these rights shall be distributed between Member States on the basis of the average percentages of beef production and, in particular, valid suckler cow premium claims as set out in the table in Annex 11.

The additional rights shall be allocated from the national reserves in the first instance to milk producers who are eligible or whose rights are increased for the first time by virtue of the first subparagraph who comply with the terms of this Regulation and who keep the eligible cows on their holding on 1 January 1993 and retain them there for six months. Any remaining part of this additional quota which is not allocated to such producers may be allocated according to the normal criteria for use of the national reserve. Should the total number of additional rights to be allocated exceed the number of additional rights available by virtue of Annex 11, the Member State concerned may reduce, proportionately, all the applications for additional rights or give priority to certain producers, according to objective criteria to be determined.

In allocating the amounts to producers for whom the maximum number of eligible cows was previously limited to ten, any quota rights established by such producers under Article 4d (2) shall be taken into account. The reduction provided for in paragraph 2 shall apply in the same way to the ceilings laid down or to the increases in the ceiling established in accordance with the foregoing subparagraph.

The fact of whether cows belong to a suckler herd or to a dairy herd shall be checked on the basis of the beneficiary's reference quantity and an average milk yield to be fixed in accordance with the procedure laid down in Article 27.

7.   Per eligible animal, the amount of the premium shall be:

ECU 70 for the 1993 calendar year,

ECU 95 for the 1994 calendar year,

ECU 120 for the 1995 calendar year and thereafter.

Save in duly justified exceptional cases, payment must be made as soon as the inspections are carried out and not later than 30 June of the year following the calendar year in respect of which the premium is applied for.

Member States may grant an additional national premium, up to a maximum of ECU 25 per cow, provided that no discrimination is caused between stockfarmers in the Member State concerned.

In respect of holdings located in a region as referred to in the Annex of Regulation (EEC) No 2052/88 the first ECU 20 per cow of this additional premium shall be financed by the Guarantee Section of the European Agricultural Guidance and Guarantee Fund (EAGGF).

The preceding subparagraph shall be extended to holdings situated throughout the territory of a Member State if in the Member State concerned the cattle population has a high proportion of suckler cows, representing at least 30% of the total number of cows, and if at least 30% of male bovine animals slaughtered belong to conformation classes S and E. Any overshoot of these percentages is established on the basis of the average of the two years preceding that for which the premium is granted.

8.   Detailed rules for the application of this Article shall be adopted by the Commission in accordance with the procedure laid down in Article 27:

> – in particular those allowing the Member States to determine taking into account the structure of their herds of suckler cows, the reduction referred to in paragraph 2,
>
> – and also those relating to the definition of the concept of suckler cow referred to in Article 4a.

Article 4e

1.   Where a producer sells or otherwise transfers his holding, he may transfer all his suckler cow premium rights to the person taking over his holding. He may also transfer, in full or in part, his rights to other producers without transferring his holding. In accordance with the procedure laid down in Article 27, the Commission may lay down specific rules relating to the minimum number which may form the subject of a partial transfer.

In the case of transfer without transfer of the holding a part of the transferred rights, which shall not exceed 15%, shall be returned without compensatory payment to the national reserve of the Member State where his holding is situated to be distributed free of charge to newcomers or to other priority producers referred to in Article 4f(2).

2.   The Member States:

(a)   shall take the necessary measures to prevent premium rights being transferred outside sensitive areas or regions where beef and veal production is particularly important for the local economy;

(b)   may provide either that the transfer of rights without transfer of the holding is carried out directly between producers or that it is carried out through the intermediary of the national reserve.

3.   Member States may authorize, before a date to be determined, temporary transfers of part of the premium rights which are not intended to be used by the producer who holds them.

4.   Premium rights transferred and/or temporarily transferred to a producer shall be in addition to those which were assigned to him originally with his original ceiling.

5.   Detailed rules for the application of this Article shall be adopted by the Commission in accordance with the procedure laid down in Article 27.

These detailed rules shall concern in particular provisions enabling the Member States to resolve problems relating to the transfer of premium rights by producers who are not the owners of the land occupied by their holdings.

Article 4g

1. The total number of animals qualifying for the special premium and the suckler cow premium shall be limited by the application of a stocking density on the holding. This stocking density shall be expressed in livestock units (LU) per unit of forage area of the holding used for the animals carried on it. However, a producer shall be exempt from the application of the stocking density if the number of animals held on his holding and to be taken into account for determining the stocking density is not more than 15 LU.

2. The stocking density shall be set at:
    3,5 LU/ha for the 1993 calendar year,
    3 LU/ha for the 1994 calendar year,
    2,5 LU/ha for the 1995 calendar year,
    2 LU/ha from the 1996 calendar year onwards.

3. For determining the stocking density of the holding, account shall be taken of:
    – the male bovine animals, suckler cows, sheep and/or goats for which premium applications have been submitted, as well as the dairy cows needed to produce the reference quantity of milk allocated to the producer. The number of animals shall be converted to LU by reference to the conversion table in Annex I to Regulation (EEC) No 2328/91,
    – the forage area, meaning the area of the holding available throughout the calendar year for rearing bovine animals and sheep and/or goats. The forage area does not include buildings, woods, ponds, paths or areas used for other crops eligible for Community aid or permanent crops or horticultural crops, or areas qualifying for the same system as that laid down for the producers of certain arable crops, or subject to a national or Community set-aside scheme other than the scheme referred to in point (a) of the third subparagraph of Article 2(3) of Regulation (EEC) No 2328/91. Forage area includes areas in shared use and areas which are subject to mixed cultivation under rules to be adopted in accordance with the procedure laid down in Article 27.

4. Bovine animals for which the special premium or the suckler cow premium is granted must be identified by appropriate marking. Identification data shall be entered in a special register kept by the producer.

4.(a) Member States may apply appropriate environmental measures which correspond to the specific situation of the land used for the production of male bovine animals or suckler cows qualifying for premiums. Member States which avail themselves of this possibility shall decide the penalties which are appropriate and proportional to the seriousness of the ecological consequences of not observing the said measures. These penalties may provide for a reduction or, where appropriate, cancellation of the benefits accruing from the premium schemes. Member States shall inform the Commission of the measures taken to apply this provision.

5.   The Commission shall adopt detailed rules for applying this Article in accordance with the procedure laid down in Article 27 and in particular those enabling improper application of the stocking density to be prevented.

Commission Regulation 3886/92 (OJ 1992 L391/20)†
Article 33
Use of rights
1.   A producer holding rights may make use of them by either availing himself of those rights and/or leasing those rights to another producer.
2.   Where a producer has not made use of at least 70% of his rights during each calendar year, the part not used shall be transferred to the national reserve, except:
    – in the case of a producer holding a maximum of seven rights to premium. Where this producer has not made use of at least 70% of his rights during each of two consecutive calendar years, the part not used during the last calendar year shall be transferred to the national reserve,
    – in the case of a producer participating in an extensification programme recognised by the Commission,
    – in the case of a producer participating in an early retirement scheme recognized by the Commission in which the transfer and/or temporary lease of rights is not obligatory, or
    – in duly justified exceptional cases.
3.   Temporary leasing shall only be in respect of whole calendar years and shall involve at least the minimum number of animals provided for in Article 34(1). Over a period of five years from the first leasing a producer, except in the event of a transfer of rights, shall recover all his rights for himself, for at least two consecutive calendar years. During the abovementioned two-year period, the producer shall not be permitted to lease out any right. If the producer does not avail himself of at least 70% of his rights during each year of this period, the Member State shall, except in duly justified exceptional cases, transfer annually to the national reserve that part of the rights not used by the producer.
However, for producers participating in early retirement schemes or who have, prior to the entry into force of Commission Regulation (EC) No 1719/94, undertaken to participate in extensification programmes recognised by the commission, Member States may provide for an extension of the total duration of the temporary lease on the basis of such programmes. Producers who, subsequent to the entry into force of Regulation (EC) No 1719/94, undertake to participate in an extensification programme in accordance with the measure referred to in article 2(1)(c) of council Regulation (EEC) No 2078/92 shall not be authorized to temporarily lease and/or to transfer their rights throughout the period of that participation. However, this provision shall not apply:
    – in cases where the extensification programme permits the transfer and/ or temporary lease of rights to producers whose participation in the measures other than the extensification measure referred to in Article 2 of Regulation (EEC) No 2078/92 requires the acquisition of rights,
    – to producers able to prove to the satisfaction of the competent authorities that, prior to the entry into force of Regulation (EC) No 1719/94, they had

---

† Amended in this respect by Reg 1846/95 (OJ 1995 L177/28) and Reg 2311/96 (OJ 1996 L313/9).

already notified those authorities of the transfer and/or temporary lease of rights in accordance with Article 34(2).

4.   In respect of 1997 and 1998, the figure of 70% mentioned in paragraph 2 and the first sub-paragraph of paragraph 3 shall be replaced by the figure of 90%. In this case, the rights transferred to the national reserve shall not be reallocated for 1998 or 1999.

Appendix 4

Sheep Annual Premium Scheme

Regulation 3493/90 (OJ 1990 L337/7)†
Article 1
For the purposes of this Regulation:
1. "sheepmeat and/or goatmeat producer" means: an individual farmer, whether a natural or a legal person, who, on a permanent basis, assumes the risks and/or organizes the rearing of at least 10 ewes or, in the case of the areas referred to in Article 5(5) of Regulation (EEC) No 3013/89, 10 ewes and/or she-goats within the territory of a single Member State. For the purposes of applying this Regulation, the farmer is the owner of the flock, except for special cases still to be determined which arise from contractual forms provided for in agricultural law or covered by national customs and practices under which the farmer, while assuming the risks and/or organisation of the rearing, is not the owner of all or part of the flock;
2. "producer group" means: any form of group, association or cooperation involving reciprocal rights and obligations between producers of sheepmeat and/or goatment. Associations the object of which is the joint rearing of the flock in such a manner that ownership of it cannot be attributed to its members individually are also considered to be producer groups, provided that it is established that those members personally assume the risks and/or the organization of rearing;
3. "holding" means: all production units managed by the producer or made available to him and located within the territory of one and the same Member State.
4. "eligible ewe" means: any female of the ovine species having lambed at least once or aged at least one year;
5. "eligible she-goat" means: any female of the caprine species having kidded at least once or aged at least one year.';
The Commission shall, acting in accordance with the procedure laid down in Article 30 of Regulation (EEC) No 3013/89, adopt the implementing provisions for this Article and in particular for the special cases referred to in point 1 thereof and the arrangements for fixing the limits provided for in Article 5(7) of Regulation (EEC) No 3013/89 with regard to the producer groups.

† Amended by Reg 2070/92 (OJ 1992 L215/63) and Reg 233/94 (OJ 1994 L30/9).

Commission Regulation 2700/93 (OJ 1993 L245/99)†

Article 1 – Applications

1.   In addition to the requirements under the integrated management and control system relating to certain Community aid schemes, pursuant to Regulations (EEC) No 3508/92 and (EEC) No 3887/92, producers must indicate in the premium applications whether they are marketing sheep's milk, or milk products based on sheep's milk, during the marketing year in respect of which the premium is requested.

2.   Applications for a premium in favour of sheepmeat and goatmeat producers shall be submitted to the authority designated by the Member State in the territory in which the holding is situated during a fixed period within a period commencing on 1 November preceding the commencement of the marketing year and ending on 30 April following the commencement of the marketing year in respect of which the applications are submitted.

However in the case of Italy, premium applications may be centralized; in this case the authority designated by the Member State in the territory in which the holding is situated shall receive a copy of each application.

Instead of one period, Member States may decide on two non-consecutive periods for the submission of applications within the above period. In that event, a producer in such Member States may submit his premium application only during one of the two periods.

However, the United Kingdom may set one (or two) different period(s) in respect of Northern Ireland from that (those) set for Great Britain.

3.   The retention period during which the producer undertakes to keep on his holding, within the meaning of Article 1(3) of Regulation (EEC) No 3493/90, the number of ewes and/or she goats in respect of which the premium is requested shall be 100 days starting on the last day of the period for the submission of applications referred to in paragraph 2.

Before all or some of that number of ewes and/or she goats in respect of which the premium is requested are placed in agistment during the retention period, the animals concerned must be identified. Furthermore, as from the 1995 marketing year, the place (or places) of retention must be indicated in the premium application as well as, where applicable, the period (or periods) concerned. In the event of a change of place or date relating to that period, the producer shall give prior written notification thereof to the competent authority.

Article 3(4) of Council Regulation (EEC, Euratom) No 1182/71 shall not apply for the determination of the aforesaid 100-day period.

4.   Each application shall cover at least 10 ewes and/or goats.

Article 2 – Notification

Member States shall notify the Commission:

---

† Amended by Reg 80/94 (OJ 1994 L16/1) and Reg 279/94 (OJ 1994 L37/1), Reg 2946/95 (OJ 1995 L308/26) and Reg 1526/96 (OJ 1996 L190/21).

– by 31 July of each year at the latest of the information relating to premium applications submitted during the period referred to in Article 1(2). For that purpose they shall use the model form included in Annex 1.

– by 31 July of the year following the abovementioned period, of the information relating to the number of ewes which qualified for the premium for lambs fattened as heavy carcases during the period referred to in Article 1(2). For that purpose they shall use the model form included in Annex II.

The information referred to in the above indents shall be made available to the national bodies responsible for drawing up official statistics in the sheepmeat and goatmeat sector, at their request.

Article 3

This Regulation shall enter into force on the day following its publication in the Official Journal of the European Communities.

It shall apply to applications for premiums presented for the 1996 marketing year and subsequent years.

This Regulation shall be binding in its entirety and directly applicable in all Member States.

Commission Regulation 3567/92 (OJ 1992 L362/41)†

Article 6

Where a producer has obtained premium rights free of charge from the national reserve and except in duly justified exceptional cases, he shall not be authorized to transfer and/or temporarily lease his rights during the three following marketing years.

Article 6a

1.   A producer holding rights may make use of them by either availing himself of those rights and/or by leasing those rights to another producer.

2.   Where a producer has not made use of at least 70% of his rights during each marketing year, the part not used shall be transferred to the national reserve except:

    – in the case a producer participating in an extensification programme recognized by the Commission.

    – in the case a producer participating in an early retirement scheme recognized by the Commission in which the transfer and/or temporary lease of rights is not obligatory, or

    – in duly justified exceptional cases.

3.   Temporary leasing shall only be in respect of whole marketing years and shall involve at least the minimum number of animals provided for in Article 7(1). At the end of each period of temporary leasing which may not exceed three consecutive marketing years, a producer, except in the event of a transfer of rights, shall recover all his rights for himself, for at least two consecutive years. If the producer does not avail himself of at least 70% of his rights during each of the two marketing years, the Member State shall, except in duly justified exceptional cases, retain and transfer annually to the national reserve that part of the rights not used by the producer.

However, for producers participating in early retirement schemes or who have, prior to the entry into force of Commission Regulation (EC) No 1720/94 undertaken to participate in extensification programmmes recognized by the Commission, Member States may provide for an extension of the total duration of the temporary lease on the basis of such programmes.

Producers who, subsequent to the entry into force of Regulation (EC) No 1720/94 undertake to participate in an extensification programme in accordance with the measure referred to in Article 2(1) (c) of Council Regulation (EEC) No 2078/92 shall not be authorized to temporarily lease and/or to transfer their rights throughout the period of that participation. However, this provision shall not apply:

    – in cases where the extensification programme permits the transfer and/or temporary lease of rights to producers whose participation in the

†Amended by Regs 1199/93 (OJ 1993 L122/26), 2869/93 (OJ 1993 L262/28), 3534/93 (OJ 1993 L321/13), 826/94 (OJ 1994 L95/8), 1720/94 (OJ 1994 L181/6), 2527/94 (OJ 1994 L269/11), 1847/95 (OJ 1995 L177/32), 122/97 (OJ 1997 L22/18) and 1303/97 (OJ 1997 L177/7).

measures other than the extensification measure referred to in Article 2 of Regulation (EEC) No 2078/92 requires the acquisition of rights,

– to producers able to prove to the satisfaction of the competent authorities that, prior to the entry into force of Regulation (EC) No 1720/94, they had already notified those authorities of the transfer and/or temporary lease of rights in accordance with Article 7(2).

Article 7

1.   The minimum number of premium rights which may be the subject of a partial transfer not involving the transfer of a holding shall be:

– ten rights in the case of producers holding at least 100 premium rights,
– five rights in the case of producers holding at least 20 and not more than 99 rights.

In the case of producers holding less than 20 rights, no minimum is set.

2.   Transfers of premium rights and temporary leasing of such rights shall be effective only after they have been notified to the competent authorities of the Member State by the producer transferring and/or leasing the rights and by the producer receiving the rights.

Such notification shall be within a deadline set by the Member State and not later than the date on which the premium application period ends in that Member State except in those cases where the transfer of rights takes effect through an inheritance. In that case, the producer who receives the rights must be in a position to furnish appropriate legal documents to prove that he or she is the beneficiary of the deceased producer.

3.   In the case of a transfer without a transfer of the holding, the number of rights transferred without compensation to the national reserve may in no case be less than one.

4.   Temporary leasing shall only be in respect of whole marketing years and shall involve at least the minimum number of animals provided for in paragraph 1. Over a period of five years from the first leasing a producer must, except in the event of a transfer of rights, use all his rights for himself in the course of at least two consecutive marketing years. Where one of these conditions is not fulfilled the leasing shall lapse. However, for producers participating in early retirement schemes or who have, prior to the entry into force of Regulation (EC) No 1720/94 (amending Regulation), undertaken to participate in extensification programmes recognized by the Commission, Member States may provide for an extension of the total duration of the temporary lease on the basis of such programmes.

Producers who, subsequent to the entry into force of Regulation (EC) No 1720/94 (amending Regulation), undertake to participate in an extensification programme in accordance with the measure referred to in Article 2(1)(c) of Regulation (EEC) No 1078/92 shall not be authorized to temporarily lease and/or to transfer their rights throughout the period of that participation. However, this provision shall not apply:

– in cases where the extensification programme permits the transfer and/or temporary lease of rights to producers whose participation in the

measures other than the extensification measure referred to in Article 2 of Regulation (EEC) No 2078/92 requires the acquisition of rights,
– to producers able to prove to the satisfaction of the competent authorities that, prior to the entry into force of Regulation (EC) No 1720/94, they had already notified those authorities of the transfer and/or temporary lease of rights in accordance with paragraph 2.

Article 9
In the case of transfers or temporary leasing of premium rights, Member States shall set the new individual limit and shall notify the producer concerned not later than 60 days after the last day of the period during which the producer submitted his premium application, of the number of premium rights to which they are entitled.

This measure does not apply in the case where the transfer takes effect through an inheritance under the conditions referred to in Article 7(2).

Article 10
Producers farming only public or collectively owned land who decide to stop using that land for grazing and to transfer all their rights to another producer shall be treated in the same way as producers selling or transferring their holdings. In all other cases such producers shall be treated in the same way as producers transferring their premium rights only.

Article 11
Where Member States provide that the transfer of rights without transfer of the holding is to take place via the national reserve, they shall apply national provisions analogous to those in this Title. Moreover, in such cases:
– Member States may provide for temporary leasing to be carried out via the national reserve.
–– in the event of the transfer of premium rights or temporary leasing pursuant to the above indent, transfer to the reserve shall not become effective until after notification by the competent authorities of the Member State to the transferring/leasing producer and transfers from the reserve to another producer shall not become effective until after notification to that producer by the authorities.

In addition, such provisions must ensure that the part of the rights not covered by the third subparagraph of Article 5a(4)(b) of Regulation (EEC) No 3013/89 must be offset by a payment by the Member State corresponding to the payment which would have resulted from a direct transfer between producers account being taken in particular of the trend in production in the Member State concerned. This payment shall be equal to the payment charged to a producer who receives equivalent rights from the national reserve.

Council Regulation 3013/89 (OJ 1989 L289/1)†
Article 5

1.   To the extent necessary to offset an income loss by sheepmeat producers in the Community during a marketing year, a premium shall be granted.

To this end, a single income loss shall be determined which shall be deemed to be any difference, per 100 kilograms carcase weight, between the basic price referred to in Article 3(1) and the arithmetic mean of the weekly market prices recorded in accordance with Article 4.

2.   The premium payable per ewe to the producers of heavy lambs referred to in Article 4(3) shall be obtained by multiplying the income loss referred to in paragraph 1 by a coefficient expressing for the Community as a whole the annual average production of meat from heavy lambs per ewe producing such lambs, expressed per 100 kilograms carcase weight.

3.   The amount of the premium payable per ewe to the producers of light lambs referred to in Article 4(3) shall be obtained by multiplying the income loss referred to in paragraph 1 by a co-efficient representing 80% of the coefficient determined in accordance with the provisions of paragraph 2.

4.   Each producer shall receive the premium calculated for the category in which he is classified. However, a producer marketing sheep's milk or sheep's milk products will, if he can prove that at least 40% of the lambs born on his holding have been fattened as heavy carcases with a view to their slaughter, be able, at his request, to receive the premium for the heavy category, in proportion with the number of lambs born on his holding which are fattened as heavy carcases.

5.   To offset an income loss by goatmeat producers, a premium shall be granted:

    – firstly, in the areas indicated in Annex I, and

    – secondly, in the mountain and hill areas within the meaning of Article 3(3) of Directive 75/268/EEC, other than the areas indicated in Annex I to this Regulation, provided that it is established following the procedure referred to in Article 30 that the production of those areas meets the following two criteria:

    (a) goat rearing is mainly directed towards the production of goatmeat;

    (b) goat and sheep rearing techniques are similar in nature.

The premium payable per she-goat shall be 80% of the amount per ewe in accordance with paragraph 2.

6.   Before the end of each half-year, the commission shall in accordance with the procedure laid down in Article 30 assess the foreseeable income loss for the entire marketing year and the foreseeable amount of the premium.

On the basis of this estimated income loss, the Member States shall be authorized to pay all their producers a half-yearly advance payment of 30% of the expected premium.

†Amended by Regs 3577/90 (OJ 1990 L353/23), 1741/91 (OJ 1991 L163/41), 2069/92 (OJ 1992 L215/59), 363/93 (OJ 1993 L42/1), 233/94 (OJ 1994 L30/9), 1096/94 (OJ 1994 L121/9), 1886/94 (OJ 1994 L197/30), 1265/95 (OJ 1995 L123/1), and 1589/96 (OJ 1996 L206/25).

Member States may make provision for these two advance payments to take the form of a single payment to producers as of the end of the second half-year.

The amount of the final premium shall be determined without delay after the end of the marketing year in question and not later than 31 March. Before 15 October of the same year, any balance, where appropriate, shall be paid.

Premiums shall be paid to recipient producers on the basis of the number of ewes and/or she-goats kept on their holding over a minimum period to be determined in accordance with the procedure laid down in Article 30.

7.   Until the end of the 1994 marketing year premiums for producers of sheepmeat and goatmeat referred to in this Regulation shall be paid at the full rate within the limit of 1,000 animals per producer in the less favoured areas within the meaning of Article 3(3), (4) and (5) of Directive 72/268/EEC and within the limit of 500 animals in other areas.

Outside the limits indicated in the first subparagraph the premiums payable shall until the end of the 1994 marketing year, be fixed at 50% of the amount to be calculated.

In the case of groups, associations or other forms of co-operation between producers, the limits indicated in the first sub-paragraph shall be applied individually to each of the member farmers.

8.   The Council, acting by a qualified majority on a proposal from the Commission, shall adopt general rules for implementing this Article, and in particular shall define which producers may receive the premium and for which ewes, and in the areas specified in paragraph 5, for which goats.

The Council, by the same procedure:

– may extend the premium to certain mountain-breed ewes raised in precisely defined areas presenting particularly difficult production conditions that do not qualify as eligible ewes: in such cases the premium payable shall be 70% of that for eligible ewes in accordance with paragraph 2,

– may specify that the premium is to be granted only to producers keeping a minimum number of ewes or, in the case of the areas specified in paragraph 5, a minimum number of ewes and/or she-goats.

9.   The Commission, acting in accordance with the procedure laid down in Article 30:

– shall fix as appropriate the premium payable per ewe to the producers specified in paragraphs 2 and 3 per mountain-breed female within the meaning of paragraph 8 and per she-goat in the areas specified in paragraph 5,

– shall fix for the duration of each marketing year the coefficients referred to in paragraph 2,

– shall adopt implementing rules for this Article covering, in particular, the submission of premium applications and payment of the premium.

10.   Expenditure under the arrangements provided for in this Article shall be deemed to form part of intervention for the purpose of stabilizing agricultural markets.

Article 5a

1.   An individual limit per producer is hereby introduced in respect of the grant of the premium provided for in Article 5.

In the case of producers who have been granted the premium prior to the 1992 marketing year, the premium shall be paid for the 1993 marketing year and subsequent years within the limits of the number of animals for which the premium has been paid for the 1991 marketing year, such number being multiplied by the coefficient referred to in paragraph 5.

However, where this coefficient is higher than one, Member States may decide to use, in whole or in part, the additional number of rights to the premium resulting therefrom in order to stock the reserve referred to in Article 5b(1).

These limits shall be reduced in such a way as to enable the national reserve referred to in Article 5(b)(1) to be constituted.

2.   In the case of natural circumstances which led to a non-payment or to a reduced payment of the premium for the 1991 marketing year, the number of animals corresponding to the payments made during the most recent marketing year shall be used. In the case of non-payment of the premium or of reduced payment for the 1991 marketing year, as a result of the imposition of penalties provided for to that end, the number recorded during the check which gave rise to those penalties shall be used.

3.   In the case of groups, associations or other forms of cooperation between producers, the limits laid down in paragraph 1 shall be applied individually to each associate member in accordance with the following rule:

(a)   where the group has notified the competent authority of the formula for apportioning livestock referred to in Article 2(2) of Regulation (EEC) No 2358/91 in respect of the 1991 marketing year, in accordance with Article 4 of that Regulation, those limits shall be fixed for each producer member using that formula as a basis;

(b)   where the group has not notified the competent authority of the formula for apportionment referred to in (a) in respect of the 1991 marketing year, the premium shall be paid to the group in respect of not more than the number of animals for which it was granted to the group for the 1991 marketing year, in accordance with the rules laid down in paragraph 1. An individual limit shall be fixed for each producer member in respect of the 1993 marketing year, in accordance with the allocation formula communicated by the group.

In the event of subsequent changes in the membership of the group, account shall be taken, when the premium is paid to the group, of the individual limit of each producer member who has joined or left the group.

4.(a) The right to premium attaches to producers who have been granted the premium in respect of the 1991 marketing year and who have also applied for a premium, under the 1992 marketing year.

(b)   When a producer sells or otherwise transfers his holding, he may transfer all his premium rights to the person who takes over his holding.

He may also transfer, in whole or in part, his rights to other producers without transferring his holding. According to the procedure provided for in Article 30, the Commission may draw up specific rules relating to the minimum number which could form the subject of the partial transfer.

In the case of a transfer without transfer of the holding, a part of the premium rights transferred, not exceeding 15%, shall be surrendered without compensation to the national reserve of the Member State where his holding is situated for free distribution to new entrants or other priority producers referred to in Article 5(b)(2).

However, with effect from the 1995 marketing year the previous paragraph shall not apply to groups of producers, in the case of a transfer of rights between members of the same group of producers, meeting conditions to be determined by the Commission in accordance with the procedure provided for in Article 30.

These conditions should take into account at least:
– the status of the group members,
– the length of time members have belonged to and participated in the group
– The composition of the group,
to the extent necessary not to jeopardize the application of Article 5a(4)(b), third sub-paragraph.

(c) Member States:
– must take the necessary measures to avoid premium rights being moved away from sensitive zones or regions where sheep production is especially important for the local economy,
– may provide either that the transfer of the rights without transfer of the holding is carried out directly between the producers or that it is carried out through the intermediary of the national reserve.

(d) Member States may authorize, before a date to be fixed, temporary leases of that part of the premium rights which the producer, who is entitled thereto, does not intend to use.

(e) Entitlement to the premium transferred or temporarily leased to a producer shall be aggregated with that originally granted to him.
However, the premium actually granted at the full rate shall not exceed the limits fixed in Article 5(7).

(f) The Commission shall lay down the detailed rules for implementing this paragraph in accordance with the procedure provided for in Article 30, and in particular those rules which enable Member States to determine, bearing in mind the structure of their flocks, the reduction referred to in paragraph 1 and those enabling Member States to resolve specific problems linked to the transfer of premium rights by producers who do not own the areas on which their holdings are situated.

5. For the purpose of applying paragraph 1, Member States shall establish a single coefficient representing the ratio between:

(a)   the total number of eligible animals conferring entitlement to the premium present at the beginning of one of the 1989, 1990 or 1991 marketing years on the holdings of beneficiaries, and

(b)   the total number of eligible animals conferring entitlement to the premium for the 1991 marketing year.

Member States shall inform the Commission before 31st October 1992 of the year which they have chosen for the purpose of point (a) above.

6.   Member Sates shall recalculate the individual limits in such a way that quantities above the limits of 500 and 1,000 referred to in Article 5(7) are reduced by 50%. These recalculated limits shall apply with effect from the 1995 marketing year.

Commission Regulation 2385/91 (OJ 1991 L219/15)†

Article 1

1.   Save as otherwise provided for in paragraph 4, in cases other than those referred to in Article 2(1) where ownership of a flock of sheep and/or goats on the same farm is shared between two or more natural or legal persons, the producer within the meaning of point 1 of Article 1 (1) of Regulation (EEC) No 3439/90 shall be deemed to be the person who has the greatest share of he sale of products from the flock in question.

2.   Where the owner of a flock of sheep and/or goats places the flock in agistment, the farmer in question shall remain the producer within the meaning of point 1 of Article 1 (1) of Regulation (EEC) No 3493/90. He shall identify the agister's holding in his premium application.

3.   Where a flock of ewes and/or she-goats is held, in part or in whole, under a livestock lease and the lessee receives the product of the sale of the livestock products, the lessee shall be deemed to be the producer, with regard to the part in question, within the meaning of point 1 of Article 1 (1) of Regulation (EEC) No 3493/90.

4.   Where the shepherd of a flock of sheep and/or goats is an employee of a producer within the meaning of point 1 of Article 1 (1) of Regulation (EEC) No 3493/90 and at the same time is himself a producer within the meaning of the same Article with regard to a part of the flock, the shepherd shall be jointly and severally liable with the other producer where the penalties provided for in Commission Regulation (EEC) No 3887/92 are applied in the event of the two parts of the flock not being identified separately.

The premium application submitted by each producer must specify the employer-employee relationship and identify the other producer.

Article 2

1.   Where a premium application is submitted by a producer group within the meaning of point 2 of Article 1 (1) of Regulation (EEC) No 3493/90, the producer group must submit a single premium application, which must be signed by all the producers within the meaning of point 1 of the said Article; such producers shall remain subject to the obligations imposed by Regulation (EEC) No 3007/84. The premium shall be paid directly to the group.

The rules on penalties referred to in Article 10 of Regulation (EEC) No 3887/92 shall apply to the group as such. However, the penalty provided for in that Article in the event of a false declaration intentionally made shall apply to those members who, while remaining producers in the following year, no longer form part of the group.

2.   Premium applications must state the number of animals brought to the group by each producer.

However, where the nature of the group is such that ownership of individual animals cannot be assigned to each producer, the articles of association or the

† Amended by Reg 3676/91 (OJ 1991 L349/14) and Reg 826/94 (OJ 1994 L95/8).

rules of procedure of the group must necessarily give a formula for apportioning the sheep and/or goat flock between the various producers concerned within the meaning of point 1 of the first paragraph of Article 1 of Regulation (EEC) No 3493/90.

That formula must correspond to the way the group's assets would be apportioned between the producer members were the group to be disbanded and shall be notified to the competent authority. This formula shall remain unaltered in subsequent marketing years unless the structure of the group which has been notified to the authority competent for granting the premium undergoes a substantial change; such a change shall be the result of:

– new members joining or old members leaving, or
– a change of 10% or more in the apportionment of the members' assets as a whole

Annual premium applications must specify the number of ewes attributed to each producer on the basis of the said formula.

Commission Regulation 2134/95 (OJ 1995 L214/13)

Article 1

1.   To be eligible under the fourth subparagraph of Article 5a (4) (b) of Regulation (EEC) No 3103/89, members concerned of the same producer group must meet the following conditions:

— they must continue to be members of the group for at least the three marketing years following that in respect of which the transfer of rights is notified by the producer surrendering his rights;

— they must have the status of producers as defined in Article 1 of Council Regulation (EEC) No 3493/90 and fulfil the obligations laid down in Article 2 of Commission Regulation (EEC) No 2385/91 throughout the abovementioned period.

However, the above conditions shall not apply where, during the said period, the producer concerned transfers to another member of the group his remaining rights with his holding.

Furthermore, the Member States shall lay down additional conditions where necessary to avoid jeopardizing the application of the third subparagraph of Article 5a(4)(b) of Regulation (EEC) No 3013/89; they shall inform the Commission thereof.

2.   Where, during the period referred to in paragraph 1, it is observed that at least one of the conditions laid down therein is not fulfilled, the third subparagraph of Article 5a(4)(b) of Regulation (EEC) No 3013/89 shall apply as from the marketing year during which failure to fulfil the condition(s) is observed; in such cases, the Member States shall immediately recover the corresponding rights. This measure shall apply without prejudice to additional penalties laid down nationally.

3.   By 30 April each marketing year, the Member States shall notify the Commission of the number of producers and of animals falling within the scope of paragraph 1 during the preceding marketing year and, where applicable, the penalties as referred to in paragraph 2 and the number of rights recovered where such penalties are applied.

Appendix 5

Arable Area Payment Scheme

Council Regulation 1765/92 (OJ 1992 L181/12)†
Article 1
1.   This Regulation hereby establishes a system of compensatory payments for producers of arable crops.
2.   For the purposes of this Regulation:
     the marketing year shall run from 1 July to 30 June,
     "arable crops" are taken to mean those listed in Annex 1.
Article 2
1.   Community producers of arable crops may apply for a compensatory payment under the conditions set out in this Title
2.   The compensatory payment shall be fixed on a per hectare basis and regionally differentiated.
The compensatory payment is granted for the area which is down to arable crops or subject to setaside in accordance with Article 7 of this Regulation and which does not exceed a regional base area. This is established as the average number of hectares within it down to arable crops or where appropriate fallowed in conformity with a publicly funded scheme during 1989, 1990 and 1991. A region in this sense should be understood to mean a Member State or a region within the Member State, at the option of the Member State concerned.
Where an area is not the subject of an application for aid under this Regulation but is used to justify an application for aid under Regulation (EEC) No 805/68 the said area shall be substracted from the regional base area for the period in question.
3.   Instead of a system of regional base areas a Member State may apply an individual base area system for all of its territory. A base area for each holding is established as the average number of hectares which were down to arable crops, or which were fallowed in conformity with a publicly funded scheme, during 1989, 1990 and 1991. However, where a producer alters the use to which his areas are put, his base area shall be reduced at his request.

† Amended by Reg 3738/92 (OJ 1992 L380/24), Reg 364/93 (OJ 1993 L42/3), Reg 1552/93 (OJ 1993 L154/19), Reg 231/94 (OJ 1994 L30/2), Reg 232/94 (OJ 1994 L30/7), 1994 Act of Accession (OJ 1994 C241/9), Reg 3116/94 (OJ 1994 L330/1), Reg 1460/95 (OJ 1995 L144/1), Reg 1664/95 (OJ 1995 L158/13), Reg 2800/95 (OJ 1995 L291/1), Reg 2989/95 (OJ 1995 L312/5), Reg 1575/96 (OJ 1996 L206/1), Reg 922/97 (OJ 1997 L133/1) and Reg 1422/97 (OJ 1997 L196/18).

For the purposes of establishing individual base areas, areas used with a view to taking advantage of the provisions of Regulation (EEC) No 805/68 shall not be taken into account.

4.   Where an initial choice is made for the scheme referred to in paragraph 2, subsequent recourse to the scheme referred to in paragraph 3 shall be authorized.

5.   The compensatory payment shall be granted under:

(a)   a "general scheme" open to all producers, or

(b)   a "simplified scheme" open to small producers.

Producers applying for the compensatory payment under the general scheme shall be subject to an obligation to set aside part of the land of their holding from production and shall receive a compensation for this obligation.

6.   In the case of a regional base area, when the sum of the individual areas for which aid is claimed under the arable producers' scheme, including the set-aside provided for under that scheme and land counted as being setaside pursuant to Article 7(2) is in excess of the regional base area, the following will be applied in the region in question:

– during the same marketing year, the eligible area per farmer will be reduced proportionately for all the aids granted under this Title,

– in the following marketing year, producers in the general scheme will be required to make, without compensation, an extraordinary set-aside. The percentage rate for extraordinary set-aside shall be equal to the percentage by which the regional base area has been exceeded, established by deducting 85% of the area set aside under voluntary set-aside in accordance with Article 7(6). This shall be additional to the set-aside requirement given in Article 7. However, if the excess in the regional base area leads to a level of extraordinary set-aside of less than 1% being applied in respect of the 1996 harvest, the extraordinary set-aside shall not be applied.

Areas which are the subject of extraordinary set-aside in accordance with the second indent of the preceding subparagraph shall not be taken into account in applying this paragraph.

Should exceptional climatic conditions have affected production in a marketing year in which it is found that the regional base area has been exceeded, and should those conditions have had the effect of lowering yields to a level considerably below the normal and of causing the excess in question, then, provided that the budgetary situation so allows, the Commission may, pursuant to the procedure laid down in Article 23 of Council Regulation (EEC) No 1766/92 of 30 June 1992 on the common organisation of the market in cereals totally or partially exempt producers in the regions affected from one or both measures applicable under this paragraph.

7.   Without prejudice to Article 3, where a Member State has chosen to establish one or more national base areas, it may subdivide each national base area into sub-base areas of a minimum size to be determined established pursuant to paragraph 2.

For the purposes of applying this paragraph, the "Secano" and "Regadió" base areas shall be considered as national base areas.

By way of derogation from the first subparagraph, Member States may establish, in accordance with detailed rules to be determined pursuant to the procedure provided for in Article 12, individual sub-base areas established on the basis of objective references.

Where there is an overshoot of a national base area, the Member State concerned may, in accordance with objective criteria, concentrate the measures applicable under paragraph 6 totally or partially on the sub-base areas for which the overshoot has been noted.

The Member State which has decided to apply the possibilities provided for in this paragraph shall notify producers and the Commission by 15 May of its choices and the detailed rules for their application. However, for the 1997/98 marketing year, that date shall be postponed to 15 September 1997.

Where the provisions provided for in this paragraph are applied, the consequences must be the same as those that would result from application at national level.

If the option provided for in the first subparagraph is applied, the expression "regional base area" shall, for the purposes of Article 5(1)(f) be understood to mean a sub-base area.

Article 6

From the 1993/94 marketing year onwards, the compensatory payment per hectare of protein crops is ECU 78.49 multiplied by the regional yield for cereals excluding maize yields in those regions where a separate yield is applied for maize.

Article 6a

1   A compensatory payment per hectare shall be granted for linseed.

2.   For the 1993/94 marketing year, this payment shall be set at ECU 85 multiplied by the regional yield of cereals, established by excluding the yield from maize in those regions in which a separate yield is applied for maize.

Should the area cultivated in the Community with a view to harvesting in 1993 exceed 266,000 hectares, the compensatory payment will be reduced in proportion to the excess. The granting of the said payment shall not be subject to a set-aside obligation.

3.   For the subsequent marketing years, the compensatory payment shall be set in accordance with the procedure provided for in Article 43(2) of the Treaty.

4.   The compensatory payment shall be granted only if the linseed is produced from seeds of flax varieties considered as other than those intended mainly for the production of fibres referred to in Article 1 of Regulation (EEC) No 1308/70.

Article 7

1.   The set-aside requirement for each producer applying for compensatory payments under the general scheme is fixed:

   – in the case of a regional base area, as a proportion of his area down to the arable crops concerned and for which a claim is made, and left in set-aside, pursuant to this Regulation,

   – in the case of an individual base area, as a percentage reduction of his relevant base area.

The set-aside requirement shall be 17.5%.

2.   In the case of a farm where there are areas set aside in compliance with Article 2 of Regulation (EEC) No 2328/91 these areas cannot be used to fulfill the set-aside requirement given in paragraph 1. Without prejudice to Article 9, areas set aside pursuant to Regulation (EEC) No 2078/92 which are neither put to any agricultural use nor used for any lucrative purposes other than those accepted for other land set-aside under this Regulation and areas afforested pursuant to Regulation (EEC) No 2080/92, as a result of an application made under either of those Regulations on or after the date of publication of Regulation (EEC) No 1460/95 may, up to any limit per holding which may be set by the Member State concerned, be counted as being set aside for the purposes of the set-aside requirement indicated in paragraph 1. Such limit shall be set only to the extent necessary to avoid a disproportionate amount of the available budget relating to the scheme in question being concentrated on a small number of farms.
However:
   – the compensation specified in paragraph 5 shall not be granted on these areas,
   – the compensation for income losses for land set aside in the framework of Regulation (EEC) No 2078/92 and the payment for the incentive element which are referred to in Article 5(1)(b) of that Regulation and the compensation for income losses indicated at point (c) in Article 3 of Regulation (EEC) No 2080/92 shall be limited for the areas in question to an amount equal at most to the compensation specified for that land in paragraph 5 of this Article, and
   – a Member State may prohibit or restrict transfers under paragraph 7 of a set-aside requirement to a producer who makes use of the possibility in the second sub-paragraph if such transfers would be likely to frustrate the objective of encouraging a more balanced uptake of schemes under Regulations (EEC) No 2078/92 and Regulation (EEC) No 2080/92 as between areas which comprise predominantly, or only, arable land and areas which comprise, predominantly, or only, non arable land.
Member States may decide not to apply the scheme provided for in the second sub-paragraph to a new applicant in any region in which there is a continuing risk of a significant overshoot of the regional base area.
Member States shall report to the Commission on or before 31 December 1997 on the way in which they have applied the scheme, if at all, together with the relevant statistics. On the basis of those reports the Commission shall review the operation of the scheme and shall publish a report as to its implementation and effects, on or before 30 June 1998 accompanied, if necessary, by a proposal.
3.   Member States shall apply appropriate environmental measures which correspond to the specific situation of the land set aside.
4.   The land set aside may be used for the provision of materials for the manufacture within the Community of products not primarily intended for human or animal consumption, provided that effective control systems are applied. Member States are authorized to grant national aid to producers to help them to cover the costs of planting multiannual crops for biomass production.

The aid may not, however, be more than the equivalent of the interest to be paid on a loan, repayable in five equal annual instalments, taken out for an amount not exceeding five years of compensatory payments for the land in question.

5. The compensation for the set-aside obligation shall be ECU 68.83 multiplied by the average cereal yield worked out in the regionalization plan.

Compensation shall be paid on the number of hectares needed to meet the requirement set out in paragraph 1. In the case of Portugal, compensation shall take account of the aid granted under Regulation (EEC) No 3653/90.

6. To help reduce production, producers may be granted the compensation provided for in paragraph 5 on land set aside in excess of their obligation in order to better control production. In such cases, the area set aside may not exceed the area under arable crops for which compensatory payment is requested. In this connection, the special set-aside referred to in Article 2(6) shall be regarded as an area under arable crops for which compensatory payment is required. Member States may prescribe a lower set-aside limit for a specific reason with respect to their agriculture such as protection of the environment or the risk of excessive reduction of farming in certain areas.

By way of derogation from the previous subparagraph, producers who, pursuant to Regulation (EEC)) No 2328/91, have set aside a greater area of land than that on which they intend to grow eligible arable crops and who have not recommenced the growing of crops on that land, may, at the end of the period of commitment referred to in Article 2(3) of the above mentioned Regulation, continue to set aside land which they had already set aside pursuant to this measure for a further period of 60 months. Payment of the set-aside shall then be established at the rate of ECU 48.30 per tonne for the portion exceeding that under arable crops for which compensatory payment is requested. In this connection, the special set-aside referred to in Article 2(6) shall be regarded as an area under arable crops for which compensatory payment is requested. This option shall also be available to producers whose set-aside requirement ended in September 1993 and who, in view of the uncertainty about future rules, have recommenced the growing of crops on that land with a view to a 1994 harvest. However, Member States shall be free not to apply this option for the same reasons as those in the previous subparagraph.

7. A producer may transfer a set-aside requirement to another producer in the same Member State.
  – if under national environmental rules a producer setting aside some of his arable land is required to reduce his livestock. The Member State may prohibit transfers across the boundaries of regions as indicated in Article 2(2),
  – under a plan presented in advance to the Commission, which shall verify that it does not affect the effectiveness of the set-aside scheme Transfers under such plans shall be restricted to a maximum distance of 20 km or be made within a particular area for which, in particular, specific environmental objectives are sought. The set-aside rate referred to in the second sub-paragraph of paragraph 1 shall be increased by three percentage points.

A Member State may decide not to apply the scheme provided for in this indent.

If the transfer is made to another yield region, the area to be set aside shall be adjusted accordingly.

The entitlement to compensation of a producer transferring his set-aside obligation shall be conditional on full execution of that obligation by the producer to whom it is transferred.

Article 8

1.   Small producers of arable crops may apply for the compensatory payment under the simplified scheme.

2.   Small producers are producers who make a claim for compensatory payments for an area no bigger than the area which would be needed to produce 92 tonnes of cereals, if they achieve the average cereals yield which has been determined for their region or, in the case of the Member States who operate the system of individual base area, whose individual base area is no bigger than that area.

3.   Under the simplified scheme:
  – no set-aside requirement is imposed,
  – the compensatory payment shall be paid at the rate applicable for cereals for all areas sown to arable crops.

Article 9

Applications for the compensatory payment and set-aside declarations may not be made in respect of land that on 31 December 1991 was under permanent pasture, permanent crops or trees or was used for non-agricultural purposes.

Member States may, on terms to be determined, depart from these provisions under certain specific circumstances, in particular for areas subject to restructuring programmes or for areas subject to standard rotations of multiannual arable crops with those crops listed in Annex 1. In such cases they shall take action to prevent any significant increase in the total eligible agricultural area. This may in particular involve deeming previously eligible areas ineligible as an offsetting measure.

Member States may also depart from the provisions of the first subparagraph under certain specific circumstances relating to one or other form of public intervention where such intervention results in a farmer growing crops on land previously regarded as ineligible in order to continue his normal agricultural activity and if the intervention in question means that land originally eligible ceases to be so with the result that the total amount of eligible land is not increased significantly.

Moreover, Member States may, in certain cases not covered by the previous two subparagraphs, depart from the first subparagraph if they provide proof in a plan submitted to the Commission that the total amount of eligible land remains unchanged.

Article 10

1.   The compensatory payments for cereals, protein crops and linseed, and the compensation granted by virtue of the set-aside obligation, shall be paid between the period 16 October to 31 December which follows the harvest.

2.   In order to qualify for the compensatory payment, a producer must, at the latest by 15 May preceding the relevant harvest:
- have sown the seed,
- have lodged an application.

3.   The application must be accompanied by references enabling the areas concerned to be identified. The areas down to arable crops and the areas set aside in accordance with this Regulation shall be shown in the form of separate entities.

4.   The Commission, in accordance with the procedure laid down in Article 23 of Regulation (EEC) No 1766/92 may decide that certain varieties of durum wheat are ineligible for the supplement referred to in Article 4(3) and (4).

5. Member States shall take the necessary measures to remind applicants of the need to respect existing environmental legislation.

Article 11

1.   Access to the compensatory payment for growers of oil seed rape and colza shall be restricted to those growers using seed of an approved quality and variety. The Commission, in accordance with the procedure laid down in Article 38 of Regulation 136/66/EEC shall establish what rapeseed and colzaseed shall be eligible for aid.

2.   Producers who apply for an oil seeds compensation payment shall be entitled to an advance payment of no more than 50% of the Projected Regional Reference Amount. Where the provisions specifically applying to Germany laid down in the penultimate sentence of Article 5(1)(f) are likely to affect the date of payment of the advance payment provided for in Article 11(2) or the amount thereof, a date for payment and/or advance payment specific to Germany may be fixed. Member States shall carry out the necessary checks to ensure entitlement to the advance is justified. Once entitlement to the payment is established, payment of the advance should be made.

3.   In order to qualify for an advance payment, a producer must by the date specified for the region in question, have sown the seed and have lodged with the competent agency of the Member State a detailed cultivation plan for this holding showing the land to be used for cultivating oil seeds.

4.   Where an advance has been made, a balance shall be paid equal to the difference, if any, between the amount of the advance and the Final Regional Reference Amount.

5.   Where a producer demonstrates that he has retained ownership of the produce for a period to be determined, an orderly marketing bonus may be payable. The amount of the bonus and the conditions determining eligibility shall be adopted by the Commission in accordance with the procedure laid down in Article 38 of Regulation No 136/66/EEC.

6.   The timetable of the regionalized system of payments to applicants shall be established by the Commission in accordance with the procedure referred to in Article 38 of Regulation No 136/66/EEC.

7. Notwithstanding the provisions of this Article, Member States in which there is a significant risk of the National Reference Area set out in Annex V being substantially exceeded in the following market year may limit the area for which an individual producer may receive the oilseed compensatory payments referred to in Article 5. Such limit shall be calculated as a percentage of the arable land area, of either the Member State or the Regional Base Area, that is eligible for the compensatory payments provided for in this Regulation and shall be applied to the eligible arable area of the producer. This limit may be differentiated between Regional Base Areas on the basis of objective criteria. Member States shall announce such limit, at the latest, by 1 August of the marketing year prior to that in respect of which the compensatory payment is requested, or by an earlier date in the case of a Member State, or regions within a Member State, where plantings for the marketing year concerned take place prior to 1 August.

Annex 1
Definition of products

C.N. Code	Description

I. CEREALS

1001 10	Durum Wheat
1001 90	Other wheat and meslin other than durum wheat
1002 00 00	Rye
1003 00	Barley
1004 00	Oats
1005	Maize
1007 00	Grain sorghum
1008	Buckwheat, millet and canary seed; other cereals
0709 90 60	Sweet corn

II. OIL SEEDS

1201 00	Soya beans
1205 00	Rape seed
1206 00	Sunflower seed

III. PROTEIN CROPS

0713 10	Peas shall be understood to mean only those peas sown with the intention of harvesting them in their dry state at full agricultural ripeness
0713 50	Field beans
1209 29 50	Sweet lupins

IV. FLAX OTHER THAN FIBRE FLAX

1204 00	Linseed (linum usitatissimum L.)

Commission Regulation 762/94 (OJ 1994 L90/8)†

Article 2

Without prejudice to Article 7(4) of Regulation (EEC) No 1765/92, "set-aside" means the leaving fallow of an area which has been cultivated in the previous year with a view to a harvest.

However, areas set aside previously under Regulations (EEC) No 2328/91 and (EEC) No 1765/92 and those set aside pursuant to Regulation (EEC) No 2078/92 or afforested pursuant to Regulation (EEC) No 2080/92 as a result of a request under one of these two Regulations from 28 June 1995 shall, without prejudice to Article 4(1) to this Regulation, be treated as areas under cultivation.

Article 3

1.   Land set aside under this Regulation must cover an area of at least 0.3 contiguous hectares and have a width of at least 20 metres. Smaller areas shall not be considered unless they involve whole fields with permanent boundaries such as walls hedges or watercourses. Member States may take into consideration entire parcels of less than 20 metres in width in regions where such parcels constitute a traditional form of fragmentation.

2.   The areas set aside must be cared for so as to maintain good cropping conditions. They may not be used for agricultural production of any sort other than that referred to in Article 7(4) of Regulation (EEC) No 1765/92, nor put to any lucrative use incompatible with the growing of an arable crop. However, these provisions shall not apply to land set aside pursuant to Regulation (EEC) No 2078/92 or Regulation (EEC) No 2080/92 counted for the purposes of the set-aside obligation if they are incompatible with the environmental or afforestation requirements imposed by those two Regulations.

3.   Member States shall apply the appropriate measures which correspond to the specific situation of the land set aside so as to ensure the protection of the environment. These measures may also concern a green cover; in that case, the measures must provide that the plant cover may not be used for seed production and that it may on no account be used for agricultural purposes before 31 August or produce, before the following 15 January, crops which are intended for commercial use.

Member States shall decide the penalties which are appropriate and proportional to the seriousness of the environmental consequences of not observing the said measures. These penalties may, in particular, provide for a reduction or, where appropriate, cancellation of the benefits accruing from the scheme provided for in Regulation (EEC) No 1765/92. Member States shall inform the Commission of the measures taken to apply this paragraph.

4.   To be considered under the scheme provided for in Regulation (EEC) No 1765/92, the areas set aside must:

---

† Amended by Reg 2249/94 (OJ 1994 L242/6), Reg 229/95 (OJ 1995 L27/3), Reg 1664/95 (OJ 1995 L158/13), Reg 2015/95 (OJ 1995 L197/2) and Reg 2930/95 (OJ 1995 L307/8).

– have been farmed by the applicant during the previous two years, save in special cases, duly justified according to objective criteria laid down by the Member State concerned, such as circumstances relating to the type of tenure, installation, or expansion of the holding by succession,

– remain set aside for a period commencing on 15 January at the latest and ending on 31 August at the earliest. However, Member States shall set the conditions under which producers may be authorized to sow seed, from 15 July, for harvesting in the following year and the conditions to be met in order for grazing to be authorized from 15 July in Member States where transhumance is traditionally practised. In addition, areas set aside under Regulation (EEC) No 2328/91 for which the commitment expires after 15 January and before 1 June may be regarded as having been set aside from 15 January under this Regulation.

5.   An area which has been set aside under Council Regulations (EEC) Nos 2078/92 and 2080/92 may not be counted for the purposes of the set-aside provided for in this Regulation.

Article 4

1.   The rotational set-aside obligation referred to in the second subparagraph of Article 7(1) of Regulation (EEC) No 1765/92 shall be regarded as met where none of the plots withdrawn has been set aside under the special set-aside referred to in Article 2(6) or under the set-aside referred to in Article 7 during one of the previous five years. However, a plot which has already been set aside may be reused if the producer has no further land available enabling him to comply with the abovementioned period.

2.   Set-aside which does not conform to the definition in paragraph 1 shall be regarded as any other form of set-aside within the meaning of the second subparagraph of Article 7(1) of Regulation (EEC) No 1765/92.

3.   Member States shall, where necessary, take steps to ensure that the set-aside of land over and above the producer's obligation, pursuant to Article 7(6) of Regulation (EEC) No 1765/92, reduces the area down to arable crops, thereby controlling production and not contributing to the base areas being exceeded.

In the light of experience the Commission will, if necessary, adopt additional rules for future marketing years in accordance with the procedure laid down in Article 23 of Council Regulation (EEC) No 1766/92.

4.   Producers must indicate on their applications for area-related aid whether the set-aside is rotational or non-rotational. However, this provision shall not apply to applications for area-related aid submitted in 1996 for the 1996/97 marketing year.

Article 5

1.   Without prejudice to Article 2(6) of Regulation (EEC) No 1765/92, producers who, under their set-aside obligation or for areas previously set aside under Regulation (EEC) No 2328/91, have opted for a form of set-aside other than rotational and who undertake to set aside the same plots for five marketing years shall receive the compensation payable under the rules in force at the time

of the commitment, without prejudice to any subsequent increase, and for the duration thereof.

2.   Where a producer has, in his area-related aid application, expressly gone back on his commitment before the end of the period referred to in paragraph 1, he must reimburse a sum equal to 5% of the compensation paid in respect of the previous marketing year for land set aside under this Article, multiplied by the number of years during which he did not comply with his original obligation.

3.   A producer who has opted for the scheme provided for in paragraph 1 may go back on his commitment without incurring the penalty provided for in paragraph 2:

(a)   in the event that he decides to submit the land in question to one of the schemes provided for in Regulations (EEC) No 2078/92 or (EEC) No 2080/92;

(b)   in special cases authorized by the Member States which entail a change in farm structure independently of the producer's will, such as land consolidation.

(c)   by informing the competent authority of it and submitting his application for area-related aid for the 1996/97 marketing year. However, parcels of land that have already benefited under the aid scheme provided for in the second subparagraph of Article 7(4) of Regulation (EEC) No 1765/92 or Articles 2(1) (g) and 10 of Regulation (EEC) No 2078/92 shall be excluded from this entitlement.

4.   If during the period of the set-aside commitment, as the result of a change in the farm's structure, the area set aside under this Article exceeds the limit laid down in the first subparagraph of Article 7(6) of Regulation (EEC) No 1765/92 the areas covered by the commitment shall be adjusted so as to observe that limit.

5.   Entitlement pursuant to this article is limited:

(a)   to producers who opted for the scheme provided for in paragraph 1 before the entry into force of Commission Regulation (EC) No 2930/95 and

(b)   producers who withdrew plots of land within the meaning of Article 7(1) of Regulation (EEC) No 1765/92 and who, in respect of this land, benefit from aid granted pursuant to the second subparagraph of Article 7(4) of that Regulation or Articles 2(1)(g) and 10 of Regulation (EEC) No 2078/92.

Article 6

Areas set aside in accordance with the second subparagraph of Article 7(6) of Regulation (EEC) No 1765/92 shall be subject to the rules laid down in this Regulation. However, if certain plots do not meet the minimum requirements laid down in Article 3(1) of this Regulation their area may be adjusted, within the holding, so that the said requirements are met.

Article 7

1.   If the declared set-aside is smaller than the area corresponding to the percentage laid down in the second subparagraph of Article 7(1) of Regulation (EEC) No1765/92, increased as appropriate pursuant to specific provisions of that Regulation, the maximum area eligible for compensatory payments to

producers of arable crops shall be calculated on the basis of the declared area set aside and pro rata to the various crops.

Article 10

1.   Producers who transfer all or part of their obligation to another producer must indicate in their application for area-related aid the identity of the producer who is actually setting the land aside, together with the basis on which the transfer is being made. Producers to whom set-aside is transferred shall indicate the identity of the producer on whose behalf land is being set aside. A set-aside obligation which is transferred in its entirety may not be performed by more than two other producers.

In the case of partial transfers, only one other producer may perform the obligation transferred.

2.   Where a set-aside obligation is transferred in accordance with Article 7(7) of Regulation (EEC) No 1765/92, the total area set aside on the holding to which the set-aside is transferred may not exceed the limit laid down in the first subparagraph of Article 7 (6) of Regulation (EEC) No 1765/92

3.   In the event of a transfer, the Member State shall pay the producers concerned the compensatory payments and/or the compensation due in respect of the areas down to arable crops and the areas set aside on their respective holdings.

4.   Without prejudice to the second subparagraph of Article 7(7) of Regulation (EEC) No 1765/92, the area to be set aside which corresponds to a transferred obligation shall be assessed in terms of the form of set-aside practised on the ho(ding to which the set-aside is transferred.

5.   In the event of a partial transfer that part of the set-aside obligation which is not transferred shall be subject to the rules governing non-rotational set-aside.

6.   Where this Article applies, the producers involved may not simultaneously transfer their obligation and perform another producer's obligation in respect of the same marketing year.

7.   In the event of transfer, a producer may not perform a set-aside obligation on behalf of more than one other producer.

8.   Producers covered by the simplified scheme may not perform the set-aside obligation on behalf of another producer.

9.   For the purposes of the second indent of the first subparagraph of Article 7(7) of Regulation (EEC) No 1765/92, the maximum radius of 20 km shall be measured from:

  – the farmstead on the holding or, failing that
  – the covered area on the holding where the main agricultural machinery is stored.

Appendix 6

Integrated Administration and Control System

Council Regulation 3508/92 (OJ 1992 L355/1)†
Article 1

1.   Each Member State shall set up an integrated administration and control system, hereinafter referred to as the "integrated system", applying:
(a)   in the crop sector:
    – the support system for producers of certain arable crops established by Regulation (EEC) No 1765/92
    – the specific measure in respect of certain grain legumes established by Regulation (EC) No 1575/96 (sic) – should probably be 1577
(b)   in the livestock sector:
    – to the premium arrangements for beef and veal producers established by Articles 4(a) to (h) of Regulation (EEC) No 805/68,
    – to the premium arrangements for sheepmeat producers introduced by Regulation (EEC) No 3013/89
    – to the specific measures for farming in mountain, hill and certain lessfavoured areas introduced by Regulation (EEC) No 2328/91 concerning compensatory allowances for cattle, sheep, goats and equidae,
hereinafter referred to as "Community schemes".
2.   The Council may, acting by a qualified majority on a Commission proposal, extend the scope of the integrated system to other Community aid schemes.
3.   For the purposes of applying Community aid schemes not covered by this Regulation and notwithstanding the specific provisions laid down under such schemes, in particular those concerning the terms under which aid may be granted, the Member States may incorporate in their administration and control mechanisms one or more of the administrative, technical or dataprocessing components of the integrated system.
Member States may extend this possibility to national schemes. They may use the information from the integrated system for statistical purposes.
Before availing themselves of these possibilities, Member States shall inform the Commission of their intentions in good time.

† Amended by Regs 165/94 (OJ 1994 L24/6), 3233/94 (OJ 1994 L338/13), 3235/94 (OJ 1994 L338/16), 1577/96 (OJ 1996 L206/4) and 2466/96 (OJ 1996 L335/1).

The Commission shall ensure that recourse to this possibility does not prejudice compliance with the provisions of the sectoral Regulations or of this Regulation.

4. Without prejudice to specific provisions provided for under the arrangements referred to in paragraph 1, for the purposes of this Regulation:

   – "farmer" shall mean an individual agricultural producer, whether a natural or legal person or a group of natural or legal persons, whatever legal status is granted the group and its members by national law, whose holding is within Community territory,

   – "holding" shall mean all the production units managed by a farmer situated within the same Member State's territory

   – "agricultural parcel" shall mean a continuous area of land on which a single crop is raised by a single farmer. In accordance with the procedure laid down in Article 12 the Commission shall adopt implementing arrangements for specific uses of agricultural parcels, in particular those concerning mixed crops and jointly used areas.

Commission Regulation 3887/92 (OJ 1992 L391/36)†

Article 2

1. For the purposes of this Regulation:

(a) a parcel that both contains trees and is used for crop production covered by Article 1 of Regulation (EEC) No 3508/92 shall be considered an agricultural parcel provided that the production envisaged can be carried out in a similar way as on parcels without trees in the same area;

(b) where a forage area is used in common, the competent authorities shall assign it between the individual farmers in proportion to their use or right of use of it;

(c) each forage area must be available for rearing animals for a minimum period of seven months, starting on a date to be determined by the Member State, which must be between 1 January and 31 March.

2. Member States shall take the measures necessary to avoid that the conversion of existing holdings or the creation of holdings after 30 June 1992 leads to the patently improper avoidance of the provisions relating to the individual limits on eligibility for premiums or land set-aside requirements imposed under the schemes indicated in Article 1 of Regulation (EEC) No 3058/92.

3. For the purposes of the integrated system, if a forage area is situated in a Member State other than that in which the principal place of business of the farmer using it is situated, that area shall be deemed at the request of the applicant to be part of the holding of that farmer provided:

 – it is situated in the immediate vicinity of the holding, and

 – a major part of all the agricultural land used by that farmer is situated in the Member State in which he has his principal place of business.

4. An aid shall not be granted if the amount per aid application does not exceed 50 ECU.

5. A Member State may decide to exclude from the application of certain elements of the Integrated System the specific measures established by Regulation (EEC) No 2328/91 which concern the compensatory allowances for producers in small areas as defined in Article 3(5) of Council Directive 75/268/EEC and which are implemented by way of contracts drawn up in conjunction with agri-environmental measures established in accordance with the provisons of Council Regulation (EEC) No 2078/92.

Article 4

1. Without prejudice to the requirements set out in regulations on individual aid schemes, 'area' aid application shall contain all necessary information, in particular:

 – the identity of the farmer,

 – particulars permitting identification of all the agricultural parcels on the holding, with their area, location, use and, where relevant, whether the parcels are irrigated, and the aid scheme concerned,

† Amended by Reg 229/95 (OJ 1995 L27/3), Reg 1648/95 (OJ 1995 L156/27) and Reg 2015/95 (OJ 1995 L197/2).

– a statement by the producer that he is aware of the requirements pertaining to the aids in question.

By "use" is meant the type of crop or ground cover or the absence of a crop.

Member States may require that uses not falling within the scope of the integrated system be declared under an "other uses" heading. However, the following uses shall be declared separately:

– production of forage intended for drying, whether artificially dehydrated or sundried, as referred to in Council Regulation (EEC) No 603/95.

– environmental set-aside and afforestation pursuant to Regulation (EEC) No 2078/92 or Regulation (EEC) No 2080/92 respectively, counted against the set-aside obligation.

2.(a) After the time limit for its submission the "area" aid application may be amended on condition that the competent authority received the amendments not later than the dates specified in Articles 10, 11 and 12 of Council Regulation (EEC) No 1765/92. By derogation from the second paragraph and even after the dates referred to in Articles 10, 11 and 12 of Regulation (EEC) No 1765/92 a Member State may authorize that an area be withdrawn from the Area Aid Application. The amendment must be notified in writing before any communication is made by the competent authority with regard either to the results of the administrative controls which affect the parcels in question or to the organisation of an on-the-spot check of the holding concerned.

Where agricultural parcels are concerned, amendments may be made to the "area" aid application only in particular cases that are properly documented, in particular death, marriage, purchase or sale, conclusion of a tenancy contract. Member States shall determine the conditions applying thereto. However, a set-aside or forage area parcel may not be added to parcels already declared except in cases which are duly justified under the provisions concerned and on condition that the parcel has already been accounted for as set-aside or forage area in the aid application of another farmer, the latter application being corrected accordingly.

Changes of use or aid scheme shall be permitted in all cases. However, a parcel may not be added to parcels declared as set aside.

(b) When a farmer decides during the period within which changes may be introduced, to use a parcel for a crop which falls within the scope of the integrated system which had not been used for such a crop, an "area" aid application may still be introduced with that period.

3. If an "area" aid application relates only to permanent pasture the Member State may provide that it may be submitted at the same time as the first 'livestock' aid application by the farmer in question lodged after the date laid down for the submission of the other 'area' aid applications in the Member State concerned, and not later than 1 July.

4. Set-aside declarations and crop declarations under the non-food product crop scheme shall be made along with the "area" application or comprise part of

it. However, for 1993 the Member States may set an earlier date for the submission of applications.

5.   An "area" aid application need not be submitted by farmers applying for only:

– the special premium for male bovine animals and/or the suckler cow premium who are exempted from the stocking rate requirement and do not apply for the supplement to these premiums,

– the deseasonalization premium,

– the ewe or she-goat premium.

6.   The "area" aid application of a producer who is a member of a producer group as defined at point 2 in Article 1 of Council Regulation (EEC) No 3493/90 and who for the same calendar year applies for both the ewe or she-goat premium and for aid under another Community scheme shall include all the agricultural parcels used by the Group. In such cases the forage area shall be assigned to the producers concerned in proportion to their individual limits as specified in Article 5a of Council Regulation (EEC) No 3013/89, valid on 1 January of the year concerned.

7.   For the sake of effective control each Member State shall determine the minimum size of agricultural parcel in respect of which an application may be made. However, the minimum size may not exceed 0.3 ha.

Article 5

1.   Without prejudice to the requirements pertaining to application for aid under individual schemes the "livestock" aid application shall contain all necessary information, in particular:

– the identity of the farmer,

– a reference to the "area" aid application if this has already been submitted, except in cases covered by Article 4(5),

– the number of animals of each species in respect of which any aid is applied for,

– where applicable, an undertaking by the applicant to keep these animals on his holding during the retention period and information on the location or locations where the animals will be held including, where applicable, the period or periods concerned and, for cattle, the identity numbers of the animals; when the location changes during that period the farmer is obliged to inform the competent authority in writing in advance,

– where applicable, the individual limit or individual ceiling for the animals concerned,

– where applicable, the individual milk reference quantity assigned to the farmer at the beginning of the 12 month period of application of the additional levy scheme which commences in the calendar year concerned; where the reference quantity is not known on the date on which the application is lodged, it shall be notified to the competent authority as soon as possible,

– a statement by the farmer that he is aware of the requirements pertaining to the aids in question.

The Member State may decide that some of this information need not be included in the aid application, where that information has already been communicated to the competent authority.

2.   Applications for the compensatory allowance as specified in Article 10(1)(a) of Council Regulation (EEC) No 2328/91 shall be lodged by a date or during a period to be set out by the Member State.

Article 5a

Without prejudice to the provisions contained in Articles 4 and 5, an aid application may be adjusted at any time after its submission, in cases of obvious error recognized by the competent authority.

Article 6

1.   Administrative and on-the-spot checks shall be made in such a way as to ensure effective verification of compliance with the terms under which aids and premiums are granted.

2.   The administrative checks referred to in Article 8(1) of Regulation (EEC) No 3508/92 shall include cross-checks on parcels and animals declared in order to ensure that aid is not granted twice in respect of the same calendar year without justification.

3.   On-the-spot checks shall cover at least a significant percentage of applications. The significant percentage shall represent at least:

 – 10% of "livestock" aid applications or participation declarations,
 – 5% of "area" aid applications. However, this percentage shall be reduced to 3% for area aid applications numbering more than 700,000 per Member State in the calendar.

Should on-the-spot checks reveal significant irregularities in a region or part of a region the competent authority shall make additional checks during the current year in that area and shall increase the percentage of applications to be checked in the following year.

4.   Applications subjected to on-the-spot checking shall be selected by the competent authority on the basis of a risk analysis and an element of representativeness of the aid applictions submitted. The risk analysis shall take account of:

 – the amount of aid involved,
 – the number of parcels and the area or number of animals for which aid is requested,
 – changes from the previous year,
 – the findings of checks made in past years,
 – other factors to be defined by the Member State.

5.   On-the-spot checks shall be unannounced and cover all the agricultural parcels and animals covered by one or more applications. Advance warning limited to the strict minimum necessary may however be given, although as a general rule, this should not exceed 48 hours.

At least 50% of the minimal checks on animals shall be made during the retention period. Checks may be effected outside that period only if the register provided for in Article 4 of Council Directive 92/102/EEC is available.

6.   Notwithstanding the second subparagraph of the preceding paragraph, where a special premium on slaughter or on the first placing on the market of animals with a view to their slaughter is granted in accordance with the provisions foreseen in the Commission Regulation establishing detailed rules relating to the premium regime foreseen in Articles 4a to 4k of Council Regulation (EEC) No 805/68 each on-the-spot check shall comprise.

 – verification on the basis of the private register kept by the producer that all the animals for which aid applications were submitted prior to the on-the-spot check have been kept throughout the retention period, and
 – verification that all the male bovine animals more than 30 days old present on the holding are properly identified and entered in the private register.

7.   Agricultural parcel areas shall be determined by any appropriate means defined by the competent authority which ensure measurement of a precision at least equivalent to that required for official measurements under the national rules. The competent authority shall set a tolerance margin taking account of the measuring method used, the accuracy of the official documents available, local factors (such as slope, shape of parcel) and the provisions of the following subparagraph.

The total area of an agricultural parcel may be taken into account provided that it is fully utilized according to the customary standards of the Member State or region concerned. In other cases the area actually utilized shall be taken into account.

8.   The eligibility of agricultural parcels shall be verified by any appropriate means. To this end additional proof shall be requested where necessary.

9.   Every animal covered by an application for a compensatory allowance provided for under Regulation (EEC) No 2328/91 must be held by the applicant for a minimum period of two months from the day following submission of the application.

Article 8

1.   Except in cases of force majeure, late lodgement of an aid application shall lead to a 1% reduction per working day in the amounts affected by the application, to which the farmer would have been entitled if the application had been lodged within the deadline. If the delay amounts to more than 25 days the application shall be considered inadmissible and no aid shall be granted.

For the purposes of this Article, "application" means an "area" aid application, a "livestock" aid application, an amendment to an 'area' aid application as referred to in Article 4(2) and confirmation of sowing as referred to in Article 2(2) of Commission Regulation (EEC) No 2294/92.

2.   Late submission of, or failure to submit, an application other than the "livestock" aid application concerned shall not entail reductions or exclusion from the aid schemes referred to in Article 4(5).

Article 9

1.   If the area actually determined is found to be greater than that declared in the "area" aid application, the area declared shall be used for calculation of the aid.

2.   If the area actually determined is found to be less than that declared in an "area aid" application, the area actually determined on inspection shall be used for calculation of the aid. However, except in cases of force majeure, the area actually determined on inspection shall be reduced
    – by twice the difference found if this is more than 3% or two hectares but not more than 20% of the determined area.
If the difference is more than 20% of the determined area no area-linked aid shall be granted.
However, in the case of a false declaration made intentionally or as a result of serious negligence
    – the farmer in question shall be excluded from the aid scheme concerned for the calendar year in question, and
    – in the case of a false declaration intentionally made, from any aid scheme referred to in Article 1(1) of Regulation (EEC) No 3508/92 for the following calendar year, in respect of an area equal to that for which his aid application was rejected.
These reductions shall not be applied if the farmer can show that his determination of the area was accurately based on information recognized by the competent authority.
Where a farmer has not met all the obligations incumbent on him in regard to parcels fallowed for non-food production purposes these shall, on the occasion of inspection for the purposes of application of this Article, be considered not to have been found.
For the purposes of this Article, "determined area" means the area for which all of the conditions laid down in the rules have been met.
3.   Forage areas, set-aside areas and each arable crop area for which a different aid rate is applicable shall be treated exclusively and separately for the purposes of applying paragraphs 1 and 2.
4.(a) The areas established in accordance with the provisions of paragraphs 1 to 3 for the purpose of calculating the aid shall be used for the calculation of the limit of the premiums referred to in Articles 4(g) and 4(h) of Regulation (EEC) No 805/68 as well as for the calculation of the compensatory allowance.
    The calculation of the maximum eligible area for the compensatory payments to arable crop producers shall be made on the basis of the area of set-aside land actually determined and on a pro rata basis for each crop concerned.
(b)   Where the set-aside obligation is transferred, the calculations referred to in subparagraph (a) of the maximum area eligible for compensatory payments to arable crop producers shall be made as follows:
    – on the basis of the determined area of the set-aside minus the area of set-aside transfered, for the farm where the transferred set-aside obligation is performed,
    – on the basis of the determined set-aside area including the set-aside area transferred, for the farm which has transferred the set-aside obligation.

5.   No aid shall be granted for the agricultural parcels concerned if it is established that the crops sown listed below do not meet the requirements of the respective provisions:
- rapeseed: Article 3 of Regulation (EEC) No 2294/92,
- sunflower: Article 3(a) of Regulation (EEC) No 2294/92,
- linseed: Article 6(a) paragraph 4 of Regulation (EEC) No 1765/92.

Article 10

1.   Where an individual limit or individual ceiling is applicable the number of animals shown in aid applications shall be reduced to the limit or ceiling set for the farmer concerned.

2.   If the number of an the animals declared in an aid application exceeds that found during checks the aid shall be calculated on the number of animals found. However, except in cases of force majeure and after paragraph 5 has been applied, the unit amount of the aid shall be reduced:

(a)   in cases where an application concerns a maximum of 20 animals:
- by the percentage corresponding to the difference found if this is not more than two animals,
- by twice the percentage corresponding to the difference found if this is more than two but not more than four animals.

If the difference is greater than four animals, no aid shall be granted;

(b)   in other cases:
- by the percentage corresponding to the difference found if this is not more than 5%,
- by twice the percentage, if the difference is more than 5% but not more than 20%.

If the difference found is more than 20% no aid shall be granted.

The percentages mentioned under (a) are calculated on the basis of the number declared, and those mentioned under (b) on the basis of the number found However, where it is found that a false declaration was made intentionally or as a result of serious negligence.
- the farmer in question shall be excluded from the aid scheme concerned for the calendar year in question, and
- in the case of a false declaration made intentionally, from the same aid scheme for the following calendar year.

If a farmer has been unable to comply with his retention undertaking as a result of force majeure he shall retain his right to a premium in respect of the number of animals actually eligible at the time when the case of force majeure occurred. In no case may premiums be granted on a greater number of animals than that shown in the aid application. If the compensatory allowance provided for in Regulation (EEC) No 2328/91 is calculated on the basis of livestock units the determining of the number present and the sanctions provided for above shall apply on the basis of the number of livestock units corresponding to the number of animals declared and found.

For the purposes of this paragraph animals eligible for different premiums shall be treated separately

3.   Without prejudice to the preceding paragraph where an on-the-spot check. effected by virtue of Article 6 (6) reveals that the number of animals present on the holding and for which an application is likely to be submitted does not correspond to the number of animals entered in the private register the total amount of the special premiums to be granted to the applicant during the calendar year concerned shall, except in cases of force majeure, be reduced proportionately. However:

– if the difference found during an on-the-spot check is greater than or equal to 20% of the number of animals present or if a difference of at least 3% or at least two animals is found during two checks in the same year, no premium shall be granted for that calendar year,

– if inaccurate entries in the register are found to be intentional or the result of serious negligence by the applicant in question, he shall be excluded from the special premium scheme for the current calendar year and the following calendar year.

4.   Male bovine animals present on the holding shall not be counted unless identified in the aid application, or, in the case where paragraph 3 is applied, those identified in the register.

However, a suckler cow declared for the premium or a bovine declared for the compensatory allowance provided for in Regulation (EEC) No 2328/91 may be replaced by another suckler cow or bovine respectively provided that replacement occurs within 20 days of the animal's departure form the holding and that the replacement is entered in the private register not later than three days after the day of replacement. If the compensatory allowance provided for in Regulation (EEC) No 2328/91 is calculated on the basis of the number of livestock units without distinguishing between the species of animals concerned animals declared can be replaced by other animals eligible for this allowance on condition that the corresponding number of livestock units does not decrease and that replacements take place according to the conditions provided for in the previous subparagraph.

5.   In cases where owing to the impact of natural circumstances the farmer cannot meet his commitment to keep the animals notified for a premium throughout the compulsory retention period he shall be entitled to the premium for the number of eligible animals actually kept throughout the period provided that he has informed the competent authority in writing within 10 working days of finding any reduction in the number of animals.

Article 11

1.   The penalties laid down in this Regulation shall be without prejudice to additional penalties laid down at national level.

2.   A case of force majeure with relevant evidence to the satisfaction of the competent authority must be lodged in writing with the authority within 10 working days of the date on which the farmer is in a position to do so.

3.   Without prejudice to the actual circumstances to be taken into account in individual cases, the competent authorities may recognize, in particular, the following cases of force majeure:

(a)   the death of the farmer;

(b)   long-term professional incapacity of the farmer;

(c)   expropriation of a major part of the agricultural land managed by the farmer if such expropriation could not be anticipated on the day the application was lodged

(d)   a severe natural disaster gravely affecting the holding's agricultural land;

(e)   the accidental destruction of livestock buildings on the holding

(f)   an epizootic affecting part or all of the farmer's livestock.

The Member States shall notify the Commission of the cases which they recognize as force majeure.

Appendix 7

CAP – Notes on Timing

	DEC	JAN	FEB	MAR	APR	MAY	JUN	JUL	AUG	SEP	OCT	NOV	DEC	JAN	LATER
	4	5			15										

SHEEP

Application Period

Retention Period

TRANSFER MUST BE NOTIFIED BY 4TH FEBRUARY

30% 1st Payment

30% 2nd Payment

April 3rd Payment Balance

DEC JAN FEB MAR APR MAY JUN JUL AUG SEP OCT NOV DEC JAN LATER

SUCKLER COWS

APPLICATION PERIOD   1.7 to 5.12

RETENTION PERIOD – 6 MONTHS FROM VALID CLAIM

TRANSFER MUST BE NOTIFIED BEFORE CLAIM IS MADE AND BY 5TH DECEMBER

After 1/11 1st Payment 80%

April/June Bal. Payment

BEEF

APPLICATION – Steers 1st Premium >8 months <21 months
2nd Premium 21 months+
Bulls Single Premium >8 months <21 months

RETENTION PERIOD – 2 MONTHS FROM CLAIM OR FROM SUCH LATER DATE UP TO 2 MONTHS AFTER LODGING CHOSEN BY APPLICANT

After 1/11 1st Payment 60%

April/June Bal. Payment

MILK

31/3 END OF QUOTA YEAR TRANSFERS MUST BE NOTIFIED TO IB WITHIN 28 DAYS AND NO LATER THAN 7 WORKING DAYS AFTER END OF QUOTA YEAR LEASING 1/4 TO 31/12 (normally)

DEC	JAN	FEB	MAR	APR	MAY	JUN	JUL	AUG	SEP	OCT	NOV	DEC	JAN	LATER

IACS

15th May Area Aid Application Deadline

ARABLE

15 SET ASIDE PERIOD 31

FROM 15/1 – NO GRAZING OR HARVESTING

AFTER 15/4 – MAY APPLY NON SELECTIVE HERBICIDES TO SET ASIDE – BUT IF SO, MUST NOT CUT SAS UNTIL AFTER 1ST JULY

BY 15/5 MOST CROPS MUST BE SOWN

AFTER 1/7 MAY CULTIVATE SET ASIDE TO CONTROL WEEDS

AFTER 15/7 MAY SOW CROPS ON SET ASIDE

15/7–15/8 MUST CUT GREEN COVER OR DESTROY BY 31/8 – SUBJECT TO ENVIRONMENTAL EXCEPTION

1/9–14/1 – MAY GRAZE OWN ANIMALS OR HARVEST HAY OR SILAGE FOR OWN USE FROM SET ASIDE

AFTER 15/1 FREE USE OF SET ASIDE

BY 30/9 OILSEEDS ADVANCE PAYMENT 50%

16/10–31/12 CEREAL PROTEIN LINSEED AND SET ASIDE PAYMENTS

EARLY SPRING FINAL OILSEEDS PAYMENT BALANCE

Index